Relationship Selling

D0485280

Relationship Selling

The Key to Getting and Keeping Customers

Jim Cathcart, CSP, CPAE

A Perigee Book

A Perigee Book
Published by The Berkley Publishing Group
A division of Penguin Putnam Inc.
375 Hudson Street
New York, New York 10014

Copyright © 1990 by Jim Cathcart
Cover design by Richard Rossiter

First edition: October 1990

The Penguin Putnam Inc. World Wide Web site address is
http://www.penguinputnam.com

Library of Congress Cataloging-in-Publication Data

Cathcart, Jim.
   Relationship selling: the key to getting and keeping customers/
Jim Cathcart.
      p.   cm.
   ISBN 0-399-51644-1
   1. Selling.   2. Customer relations.   I. Title.
HF5438.25.C37   1990   90-36964   CIP
658.85—dc20

Printed in the United States of America
            19   20

Contents

To Joe D. Willard, the greatest *Relationship Selling* practitioner I know

About This Book

Through over twenty years of study in the field of human interaction, Jim Cathcart has developed *Relationship Selling*, a way of building trust and cooperation that generates sales.

This concept has been presented through over one thousand seminars for hundreds of clients in countries around the world. The techniques have been successfully employed by oil service firms in the North Sea, insurance agents in Oklahoma, utility firms in Hong Kong, automotive service firms in Canada, real estate agents in Australia, hoteliers in Kuala Lumpur, and other salespeople in every conceivable industry.

One of Jim's clients used this concept to increase annual sales from $17 million to over $100 million with no increase in the number of sales-people! They later grew to $231 million in sales.

Jim Cathcart is not just a researcher who studied selling. He is a salesperson! He has sold motorcycles, mutual funds, automobiles, life insurance, club memberships, training materials, consulting services, and even doughnuts. His annual sales today are always in the hundreds of thousands of dollars.

He has trained telephone salesclerks, sellers of corporate aircraft, medical sales reps, and industrial salespeople. This varied audience has provided the perfect laboratory for testing Relationship Selling. Countless seminar participants have provided input to refine this system.

Relationship Selling is not a theory. It is a process, a system proven worldwide for over a decade, that you can learn and use to further your own success. The techniques taught in this book are not only effective, but easy to learn and use, because they are based on the application of humanistic psychology to the sales process. Relationship Selling is the natural way to sell.

Acknowledgments

A project of this size and scope can be successful only when a number of talented and caring people agree to be involved. I would like to thank the following key individuals for their contributions to *Relationship Selling*:

Paula Cathcart and Jim Cathcart, Jr.,
Lynette Cablk,
and Joey Parker.

Much of *Relationship Selling* was refined and developed in collaboration with Anthony Alessandra, Ph.D., my frequent coauthor and friend. The concept of "nonmanipulative selling" developed by Tony Alessandra and Phil Wexler added much to my six steps of *Relationship Selling*.

Many of the concepts in this book are extensions of ideas from my former works, *Relationship Strategies* (audio), *Relationship Selling* (video), *The Business of Selling* (book), and from the thousands of participants in my seminars worldwide.

Relationship Selling's initial success was greatly aided by the support of Tom Joseph of National Seminars and Bob Berg, my former Director of Sales.

Author's Note
for the 21st-Century Salesperson

Since I wrote this book many changes have taken place in the world-wide business community. Personal computers are on every desk, cellular and digital phones abound, the Internet has connected us all and satellites ring the earth with communication possibilities.

But one thing has not changed: people still want to do business with people, not "companies." The determining factor in the sale is still the person making the sale.

When there is not much difference in your product or price, there MUST be a big difference in the way you deal with people. So, whether you sell by phone, computer or video, learn and apply Relationship Selling. It will make a difference for you.

— Jim Cathcart
La Jolla, California
1997

Introduction

Relationship Selling transcends the sales transaction and looks beyond it to the ongoing relationship built between the buyer and the seller.

Recently I gave a speech to an audience of salespeople whose average sale was over five million dollars (The *average* sale!). I don't know about you, but for me a five million dollar sale is almost something out of fantasyland. As I gave my speech on sales strategies, I was studying them as hard as they were studying me. During the cocktail hour and throughout dinner, I constantly asked questions and observed their behavior to see what I could learn.

As I studied these purveyors of custom-built corporate jets, I learned something fascinating: they were not very different from the salespeople in the hundreds of other companies I have trained in Relationship Selling. The key differences were the size of each order and the sophistication of their buyers.

There are two common traits among all good salespeople: First, they love to make sales; in fact, they thrive on it. And, of equal importance, they respect their customers. These are the keys to success in Relationship Selling. Do you have what it takes?

If you truly love to sell, this book will show you dozens of ways to sell more often and more effectively. You'll learn how to:

- create *value units* that tip the buying scales in your favor;

- overcome "call reluctance";

- eliminate buyers' concerns;

- identify the "hot buttons" (dominant buying motives);

- avoid playing "objection-response ping-pong" with customers;

- generate an endless flow of potential customers who are eager to see you;

- and much more.

Your selling will become easier with each passing day, and the clients will ultimately begin calling you to initiate new sales.

But, be careful, because if you don't develop the second essential for successful selling — *respect for your customers*, then very little in this book will be helpful to you. In fact, if you don't have that second essential, I'd prefer that you get out of selling altogether.

Relationship Selling is built upon the win-win philosophy, which says that a good sale is a sale which benefits both the buyer and the seller. It attends to more than just the facts; it also considers each person's *feelings* to be important.

Relationship Selling transcends the sales transaction and looks beyond it to the ongoing relationship built between the buyer and the seller. It is based on many long standing and widely accepted practices used in psychology, human resources development, counseling, marketing, negotiations, and management.

Relationship Selling is not a new theory developed in a university environment. It is a practical strategy proven by thousands of salespeople in fields as diverse as banking, insurance, real estate, automotive, health care, hospitality, engineering, manufacturing, high technology, food service, and retail sales.

If you're tired of feeling like the "bad guy" when you try to "close" a difficult buyer, if you'd like to make selling an exciting way of providing service for others, if you'd like to find out just how good you can be, then come with me. *Relationship Selling* will change not only the results you produce in selling, but also the way you feel as you go about practicing your "art" each day.

Congratulations on the person you are about to become!

Successful Salespeople:
They love to make sales
They respect their customers

Part One

What's Different About Relationship Selling?

Relationship Selling is focused on building a good relationship with someone and providing a valuable service through that relationship.

Have you ever gone out to buy something and found exactly what you were looking for, but refused to buy it because you didn't like the way you were treated by the salesperson? Just about everyone has had this unpleasant experience at least once. We are lured into a business by great advertising and marketing only to discover that they really don't care as much about their customers as we thought they did.

None of us likes to be exploited or manipulated, and when we encounter that type of selling, we recoil. We simply don't allow ourselves to be treated in that manner.

> *Poor human relations can ruin the best marketing effort you could ever put together.*

The attitude of the salesperson can make or break a sale. What keeps a business going is not just the marketing that brings customers in the door; it's the contact with a person, the face-to-face part of selling that lets the customer know you care about him or her as an individual and that your product or service is the right product or service to meet his or her needs.

I believe selling should be a friendly act. Something we do to help people. Something we do *with* people and *for* people, not *to* them.

> *Selling is a helping profession, and that's the way it should be.*

Selling needs to outgrow its old image, to develop into a more professional approach to doing business between people. Anybody can learn to sell, and anybody can do very well *if* they can stop focusing on *me* (the seller) and instead focus on *we* (buyer and seller), working together to solve the problems or meet the needs of the buyer.

Selling Techniques

Let's play a word association game for a moment. Take out pencil and paper and write down the impressions that come to mind when you think of the word "salesman"? Don't dwell on this — just quickly jot down those images that pop into your mind.

Chances are, your list contains one or more of the old stereotypes. The image of someone who is pushy, fast-talking, aggressive, slick, wears suede shoes, and smokes a big cigar is what has been presented and reinforced by the media throughout history.

Now, that's not the way selling is in reality. When you meet people in selling, regardless of what they're selling, you often find that they are very professional, respectable people who are doing a good job in selling. But the old stereotype still exists. And there's a problem: the old type of sales training, the type that taught the aggressive, competitive style of selling in which somebody wins and somebody loses, is still present in most sales training. Many people are still being taught the same old techniques.

You know the techniques I'm referring to. The "friendly" ones like the Half-Nelson Close, the Mother-in-Law Close, the Nail Down, the Sharp-Angle Close, the Hat-in-Hand Close, and other general persuasions. The old type of selling uses such a canned routine that you feel manipulated from the very beginning. That's not how a true professional sells today, but traces of that old type of sales training continue to hang on.

Have you ever just sat down to dinner when the phone rang and it was a salesperson who immediately launched into a spiel so routine you knew he or she was just reading a script — the type that opens up with such familiarity that it's insulting to you. You know this caller doesn't know you and doesn't care to get to know you, either. That kind of approach is what I mean by old-style selling.

A seller using the old style of selling is not listening to your concerns, but simply offering a standard answer for any point you may raise. This approach is insulting, because you *know* the seller is not listening to you and you know that all potential customers receive the same answers to their concerns. The seller is not trying to help *you*.

No true professional uses this totally canned approach, but little traces of that old style of selling lurk even in the language we use as we do business today. For example, think about the word *close*. What does *close* mean to you? When I hear the word, I make these kinds of associations: "He has a closed mind," or "This is a closed meeting," or "The case is closed." None of these thoughts is particularly attractive, because they all imply "go away." All of them contain words designed to shut you out.

Yet we continue to say to each other: "Did you close anybody today?" The word itself is not a bad word, but the implication is that once you've completed the close, the transaction is finished forever. *Close* implies something we do *to* people rather than *for* people.

What we really want to do is not to close anything, but to open the relationship. Yes, we want to *confirm* the sale. But we don't want to close off the relationship. We confirm the sale by getting a check, an order, even a handshake; but we don't close anybody. The implication is too negative. A confirmation of the sale should mean that we are *opening* a relationship.

How about this one: *cold call*. It doesn't sound friendly; yet we are expected to *be* friendly. On a cold call one person walks into the home or place of business of another person, introduces himself or herself, and checks to see if there's an opportunity to make a sale that day.

Why not call it an *introductory call*? That's really what it is, because we are there for the opportunity of introducing ourselves and our company and finding out if it's appropriate to make a sale.

If it's not appropriate, guess what we should do? That's right, *go away*! And arrange to come back when it's appropriate to make a sale.

If it's appropriate to sell that day, what should we do? *Sell!* Because selling is a friendly act and a helpful act. Selling is something we do *for* someone, not *to* someone. This is the principle we want to keep in mind.

Webster's dictionary still contains some of the old, negative idioms related to selling such as, "to deliver up for sale," "to sell down the river," "to fool as if by hoax," "to betray." It contains some nicer definitions, too; but, nevertheless, the bad ones are still in there.

I think it's time selling got a better reputation. After all, *selling is a noble profession*. Selling drives the free-enterprise system!

Everytime a sale is made, our economic system thrives a little bit more. Red Motley said, "Nothing happens until somebody sells something." Good point! Selling is what causes it all to happen.

Another person put it this way:

Production − Sales = Scrap

Selling is a supportive activity that is done to *fill needs*. A salesperson's role is to go out and find where the needs are, find out which people could benefit from this product or service, and then sell in a way that is appropriate to each customer.

Developing Sales Skills

The evolution of selling has been slow, because salespeople receive no training, inadequate training, or wrong training.

In many organizations no sales training is offered. New salespeople are told about the product and how it works, shown a client list, and told to go to it. *Go to what*? They haven't been given any sales training or taught any selling skills. Yet they are expected to become successful producers! Left alone, they often watch what someone else has done to be successful. But this is hazardous, because sometimes they don't choose good role models.

In other companies new salespeople get some training, but not necessarily the right type.

In selling, you need skills in three areas: technical knowledge skills, interpersonal skills, and self-management skills (see Figure 1A).

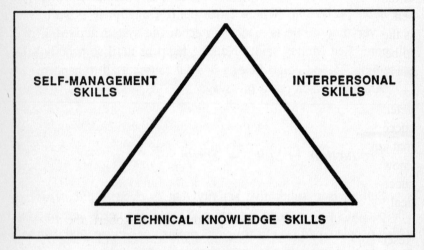

Figure 1A.   The Sales Effectiveness Triangle.

Technical knowledge means product-related knowledge. What do you know about the *technical* aspects of your product? For example, if you're selling real estate, what do you know about the property values in your area? Where is the population moving to? What are the trends in real estate at this time?

Technical knowledge is vitally important; that's why it forms the base of our Sales Effectiveness Triangle.

But just product knowledge or technical knowledge is not enough. You have to know how to *apply* that knowledge with the people you meet. This is what is meant by *interpersonal skills.*

The third kind of skill you need is *self-management skill*, the ability to manage yourself well enough to get the job done when it needs to be done, as it needs to be done. This means doing a good job whether you feel like it, or not.

Of the three skills areas, most companies continue to put most of their training dollars toward technical knowledge. The assumption is that the more you know about your product, the more of it you'll sell. But there is a dangerous fallacy in this theory. If all you know is the technical aspect of your product, you become an *educator* (not to be confused with *salesperson*). Technical knowledge is part of the basis of your success, but only part of it.

Several years ago, The Carnegie Foundation did a study to determine, across a broad range of fields, what determines a person's success. What is it that contributes to being successful? They found that only 15 percent of a person's success comes from technical knowledge! The report went on to predict that 85 percent of your success in life will be determined by a combination of your ability to deal with people and your ability to manage yourself.

According to professional speaker, Cavett Robert, the Stanford Research Institute did a follow up study several years later, again using a broad spectrum of industries. The responses were similar: Of those who were successful, only 12-1/2 percent of their success was based on technical knowledge, while 87-1/2 percent of their success came from interpersonal skills and self-management skills. If anything, the gap is getting wider all the time. So all three skill areas are essential.

Unfortunately, in some companies people are taught the *wrong* skills. Not only are they not taught the appropriate interpersonal and self-management skills, but they are taught skills and attitudes that are completely *inappropriate.*

Traditional Selling Versus Relationship Selling

There are two schools of thought in selling. The first I call *traditional selling*; the second I call *Relationship Selling*. Figures 1B and 1C show the differences between these two types of selling.

TRADITIONAL SELLING	RELATIONSHIP SELLING
The most familiar.	Less common (more valuable).
Selling is a contest.	Selling is a service.
"Selling is persuading."	"Selling is helping."
Customers must be sold.	Customers love to buy.
"Buyers are liars."	Buyers want a salesperson they can trust.
The "close" is #1.	The follow-through is #1.
Great sellers are manipulators.	Great sellers truly care.
It works — once!	*It works — again and again!*

Further Differences

TRADITIONAL SELLING	RELATIONSHIP SELLING
Canned approach	Flexible approach
One-sided	Two-sided
Sales pitch	Sales dialogue
Adversaries	Partners
Overcomes objections	Resolves concerns
Avoids phone calls	Welcomes phone calls
Persuader	Helper
Me vs. You = Fear	Me with You = Confidence
CON artist	PRO-fessional
Lonely	Fun

Figure 1B. The Two Schools of Thought in Selling

TRADITIONAL SELLING	RELATIONSHIP SELLING
"Me" oriented.	"We" oriented.
Persuasion	Communication
Showmanship	Interviewing
Aggressiveness	Questioning
Thick skin	Cooperation
Competitiveness	Sensitivity
Killer instinct	Helping instinct

Figure 1C. Skills Needed for Success in Sales

The traditional selling process is often viewed as a contest with a winner and a loser — an act of persuasion in which the buyer needs to be talked into buying. It assumes that buyers *must be sold*, because they wouldn't buy on their own.

There is a saying in traditional selling that "buyers are liars." A salesman once said to me, "I can always tell when they're lying. It's when I see their lips move." Is that a healthy attitude to have toward your buyer? I think not.

The most important part of a sale to traditional salespeople is the *close*. They go along with the assumption that great sellers are master manipulators.

Relationship Selling, by contrast, is focused on building a good relationship with someone and providing a valuable service through that relationship.

Relationship selling is less common, and therefore is seen as more valuable. People are much more willing to deal with a relationship-oriented salesperson. They're not used to that approach. They are expecting to be exploited, and here is a salesperson who is friendly, professional, and appropriate.

Relationship Selling is service oriented. It focuses on the double win, so that buyer and seller both come out of the deal as winners. It is seen as a friendly act based on the understanding that *people love to buy*, that they don't have to be sold.

Buyers want to trust the person they are dealing with. They want to trust you, your product, and your company. They will not lie to you if you establish trust with them and answer their questions appropriately.

In Relationship Selling the most important part of the sale is the follow-through, when the buyers receive the product or service they want to acquire. And the master salesperson is the one who truly *cares* about his customer.

Caring is the basis for the primary differences between personal skills used in traditional selling and those used in Relationship Selling. In traditional selling you've got to have showmanship. After all, how can you persuade someone to buy if you can't put on a good show? You need to be aggressive. You need to have a thick skin to handle all the objections you'll encounter. You must be competitive and have the killer instinct, the ability to go for the juglar. Traditional selling is "me" oriented. It goes against human nature and raises tension.

Now, what skills do you need for Relationship Selling? Certainly a different set! Relationship Selling takes the principles of psychology, counseling, and human resource development, along with common courtesy, and incorporates them into the sales proces. Skills like *questioning* skills. Very few of us have ever been taught how to ask questions. *Listening* skills. Are we really listening when the buyer tries to tell us something? We need skills that develop empathy and cooperation, not competitiveness. We need the helping instinct, not the killer instinct.

Relationship Selling is "we" oriented, not "me" oriented. It goes with human nature and lowers tension.

When you find a person who truly gets joy and personal satisfaction from helping someone else do something positive, you've
found a natural for Relationship Selling. A person who takes the
attitude of "Selling — Two Win" finds that selling becomes much
more pleasurable.

The Sales Process

Buyers have predictable concerns.

* They want to be sure they can trust you, your company, and your
  product.

* They want to be understood — their goals, fears, and needs.

* They want to be sure that the value outweighs the price.

* They fear making the wrong decision and are reluctant to make
  a change.

You know that the buyer wants to be able to trust you, your
products, and your company. You also know, even before you meet
the buyer, that he or she wants to be understood. Buyers want you
to understand their goals, fears, dreams, needs, and wants.

Also buyers are concerned about price and value. *Value* is what
your product or service is worth to them in actual use. *Price* is what
they will have to spend to acquire your product or service.

Buyers are concerned about making changes. Why? Because they
are afraid they'll make a mistake. As a salesperson, you may be a
stranger to them. Because they haven't met you before, they are
naturally concerned about doing business with you and your company.

If you know ahead of time that these are predictable buyer
concerns, why not address them early in the sales call? If you address
the buyer's concerns right away, they don't have to pop up later as
objections.

There are six basic steps used in selling whether you employ traditional selling, Relationship selling, or some other concept. The six basic steps are:

1. **Plan** — You organize your ideas, do your market research, and prepare to meet an individual client.

2. **Meet** — You make your initial contact with your client. The goal of meeting is to build a business friendship that results in low tension, high cooperation.

3. **Study** — You study the client and his or her needs until you are sure you understand the situation.

4. **Propose** — You propose solutions to this person's problems or concerns. The goal is to get the client to understand how you can be helpful.

5. **Confirm** — You make the sale official. Get some type of confirmation that a sale has taken place. It can be a check, a handshake, or an order, as long as it is something that makes the deal official and confirms the sale.

6. **Assure** — Assuring customer satisfaction means seeing to it that the buyer is truly satisfied with the product or service.

Let's examine what difference it makes how you divide your time among these six steps (see Figure 1D). Let's suppose that I am a salesman and I call on you. I didn't spend much time on planning, I greet you very quickly, I haven't studied your needs, and I launch right into my sales pitch. Will I need to spend much time on my sales pitch? Yes, I probably will. Why? Because I haven't done anything to build up to it. And the pitch had better be good if I hope to overcome my lack of preparation. I will also have to spend a lot of time confirming the sale to overcome all your objections.

Now let's take a different approach. What if I spent a lot of time on research and planning before I met with you? When we did meet, I

TRADITIONAL SELLING	SELLING STEPS	RELATIONSHIP SELLING
Low	Planning	High
Low	Meeting	High
Low	Studying	High
High	Proposing	Low
High	Confirming	Low
Low	Assuring	High

Figure 1D. Time Spent in Each of the Six Steps of a Sale.

spent time getting to know you. Then I studied your needs and wants until I was sure I really understood your concerns. If I had prepared properly, would I have to spend much time on my proposal? No. Because I would have taken the time to understand you and your needs *before* I asked for the sale. Confirming would be easy because I would have eliminated the tension and opened the door to communication. Then I could spend whatever time was appropriate assuring customer satisfaction.

A professional in selling typically spends a lot of time assuring the customer. A con artist, by contrast, spends very little time. He's out the door and on to his next "mark."

Another way to look at the sales process is through the *Sales Pipeline* (see Figure 1E). From the general public, choose a targeted market, a group of specific prospects you want to cultivate. The targeted market consists, of course, of people who are interested in your product or service. Identifying a targeted market is part of the planning phase of selling.

You make contact with a prospect from your targeted market in the meeting phase. This is when potential customers enter the sales pipeline.

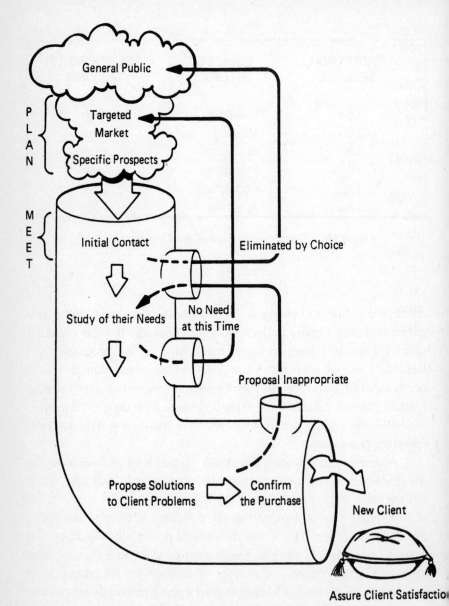

Figure 1E.   The Sales Pipeline *
*From *The Business of Selling*, Alessandra & Cathcart, Prentice-Hall

If you spend time getting to know them in this initial contact phase, you may find that some are not suited to be customers at this time. In that case, you eliminate them from your targeted market by choice. Others may have a need for your product or service in the future, but not today. In that case, they go back into the targeted market for contact at a later time.

If the prospect is still a prospect as you're moving along the pipeline and you understand his or her needs, then you turn the corner and start to propose solutions. Now is the time to show how your product or service can provide what the prospect wants and needs. If you find that your proposal is not on target, go back through the study phase until you are sure you understand the needs of that prospective customer.

When you finally get the proposal right, you confirm the sale. At that point, they come out of the pipeline as new clients. (The pillow is there to make them comfortable with that fact and to assure client satisfaction.)

Tension Levels

Let's look at how the *tension level* changes for the buyer and seller during the sales process (see Figure 1F).

During the planning phase, the buyer has no knowledge that anything is going on, so buyer tension level is low. You, the seller, on the other hand, know that future business to some degree rests on your ability to make this sale. So your tension level is moderate.

During the meeting phase, the buyer's tension level goes up because he or she wonders who you are and what you want. Your tension level is up because you want to make a good impression. The tension level for both of you should lessen as you get to know each other.

During the study phase the tension level is moderate for both of you, because you feel comfortable learning and asking questions, and the buyer feels comfortable explaining his or her needs.

Tension During the Sales Process

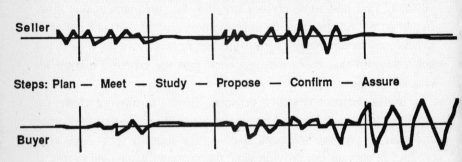

Figure 1F.   Buyer – Seller Tension Level

When you start the proposal phase, your tension level increases because you begin to think more about getting the sale, and the buyer starts to tense up, too, feeling something coming.

During the confirming phase, tension is relatively high for both parties. You want to confirm the sale, and the buyer isn't sure whether to buy or not. When the buyer finally decides to buy and places the order, you move into the assuring phase.

In the assuring phase, your tension level drops, because now you have the sale. You, as seller, are as happy as can be. But the buyer's tension level shoots off the chart, as he or she thinks, "What have I done?"

The buyer's tension in the final phase doesn't have to go to that extreme if we pay attention to how we handle each part of the sales process. A great salesperson is willing to spend time getting to know the customer and finding out how to be of help to that person.

Training magazine reported the results of a survey of sales managers who were asked to list the top problems with salespeople. Their responses identified these as the top problems:

1. Don't prospect very well.

2. Don't know competitive products.

3. Don't preplan their calls.

4. Are reluctant to make new calls.

5. Don't build strategies for working with customers.

How do you rate in these categories?

Figure 1G. Survey results

Part Two

Selling Buyers the Way They Want to Be Sold

Management and control of the tension level is one of the most effective things a seller can do to increase the likelihood of a sale. Because when tension is up, trust and cooperation are down. But when tension is down, trust and cooperation rise.

Note: Much of the material in this chapter comes from *Relationship Strategies* by Jim Cathcart and Tony Alessandra, published by Nightingale-Conant.

The single biggest obstacle to effective selling is tension between the buyer and the seller. Management and control of the tension level is one of the most effective things a seller can do to increase the likelihood of a sale. Because when tension is up, trust and cooperation are down. But when tension is down, trust and cooperation rise.

Think about the Golden Rule for a moment. I know there are several humorous versions, but I'm referring to the original: "Do unto others as you would have them do unto you."

As a salesperson, if you practice the Golden Rule exactly according to the letter, how will you do? If the other person is just like you, you'll do fine. However, if the other person is *not* like you, then you may have a problem, because he or she may not like to be treated as you like to be treated.

For example, if you're a very quick and direct person who likes to get right to the point, and you approach a somewhat shy person in this manner, you may very well scare that person away.

When a buyer and seller meet, chances are their personalities are not identical. So somebody has to adjust. Who should do the adjusting? The seller, of course! After all, you called on this person to make a sale. If, by changing your behavior, you can allow this potential buyer to remain in his or her comfort zone, your chances of a making a sale are much greater. If you insist on staying in your own comfort zone, the customer may not be able or willing to adjust. Remember, when tension goes up, cooperation and trust go down. And so do sales.

Reading Your Customer

When a person sends a message to another person, that message is *encoded* into words, phrases, or body language that is comfortable for the sender. The message can then be *decoded* according to the perceived meaning of the words, phrases, or body language as the receiver understands them. To sell effectively, early in the sales relationship you must start reading the other person and figure out *how* that person wants to be sold to.

People will teach you how to sell to them if you'll pay attention to the messages they send you.

Since the dawn of human kind, people have been trying to explain why we do what we do. Today, if you look at the information available explaining why people are different, you will find an enormous amount of data.

Several years ago, I read through piles of data with Dr. Anthony Alessandra, also a sales trainer and speaker. We concluded that there must be a way to simplify this information and boil it down into a format that can be learned and used all in the same day. To that end, we developed *Relationship Strategies*, a concept based on observable behavior.

Relationship Strategies is a practical approach to successful selling. As salespeople, we don't need to be overly concerned with the psychology of personalities. Instead we need to know how to make relationships work for us.

Relationship Strategies teaches you how to deal with different people in different ways. When you sit across from a potential buyer, you want to know what you can do to put that buyer at ease, reduce the tension level, and open communication so that you can sell your product or service and be of assistance to that customer. That's selling.

Direct and Indirect Behavior

One way to recognize the best strategy is by observing the level of directness in a person's behavior. There is a marked difference between *direct* and *indirect* behavior (see Figure 2A). On a scale from direct to indirect, very direct people seek to control circumstances, information, or other people by taking charge. They step right in and initiate action. Indirect people prefer a slower, easier going pace. They are often a little more tactful and will consider their actions carefully.

INDIRECT

Approaches risk, decisions, or change slowly and cautiously
Infrequent contributor to group conversations
Infrequently uses gestures and voice intonation to emphasize points
Often makes qualified statements: "According to my sources . . ." "I think so"
Emphasizes points through explanation of the content of the message
Questions tend to be for clarification, support, or information
Reserves expression of opinions
More patient and cooperative
Diplomatic; collaborative
When not in agreement (if it's no big deal), most likely to go along
Understated; reserved
Initial eye contact is intermittent
At social gatherings, more likely to wait for others to introduce themselves
Gentle handshake
Tends to follow established rules and policies

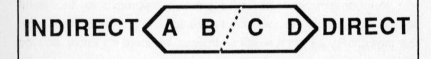

INDIRECT ⟨ A   B   C   D ⟩ DIRECT

DIRECT

Approaches risk, decisions, or change quickly and spontaneously
Frequent contributor to group conversations
Frequently uses gestures and voice intonation to emphasize points
Often makes emphatic statements: "This is so!" "I'm positive!"
Emphasizes points through confident vocal intonation and assertive body language
Questions tend to be rhetorical, to emphasize points or to challenge information
Expresses opinions readily
Less patient; competitive
Confronting; controlling
More likely to maintain his or her position when not in agreement (argues)
Intense; assertive
Initial eye contact is sustained
More likely to introduce self to others at social gathering
Firm handshake
Tends to bend or break established rules and policies

Figure 2A.   Direct and Indirect Behaviors

Direct people tend to be rather blunt and to the point. Indirect people ask you if you'd "like" to do something rather than tell you what to do.

Direct people are often risk takers, because they like to get on with their lives and their business. They like forward motion. Indirect people prefer to avoid risk, so they will take the least risky way of approaching a situation.

Looking at the scale in Figure 2A, where is home base for you? Choose the letter (A B C D) that describes your behavior most of the time and put a check mark on the scale.

Open and Self-Contained Behavior

Another behavior to observe is *openness*. Openness is a person's willingness to show what's going on inside. Open people are very relationship oriented. In a sales situation, the open person will be asking questions and making statements that focus on the two of you and the relationship you're building. The opposite of open is *self-contained*. The self-contained person is more task oriented and, in a sales situation, asks mostly questions that deal with the subject at hand, wanting to deal with business first and get to know you later. Open people are more flamboyant and outgoing. They draw attention to themselves. Self-contained people tend *not* to draw attention to themselves. Figure 2B summarizes the differences between open and self-contained behavior.

Avoid the trap of thinking that a person must be exclusively open or self-contained. Just because you are relationship oriented, doesn't mean you don't care about business. It means that when you meet people, the first thing you do is work on getting to know them and putting them at their ease. Business comes later. On the other hand, if you're a self-contained person, more task oriented, the first thing you focus on is business.

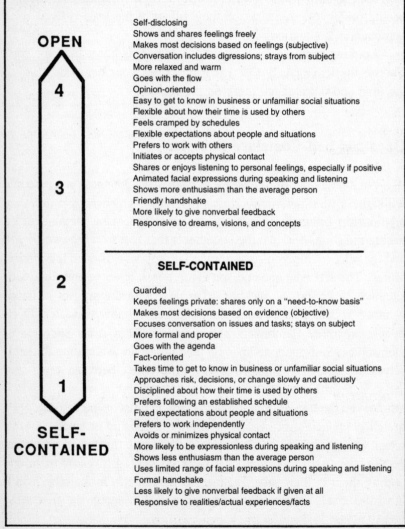

OPEN

Openness shows in the degrees of self-disclosure: the readiness and willingness to outwardly show thoughts and feelings and to accept openness from others.

OPEN

4

Self-disclosing
Shows and shares feelings freely
Makes most decisions based on feelings (subjective)
Conversation includes digressions; strays from subject
More relaxed and warm
Goes with the flow
Opinion-oriented
Easy to get to know in business or unfamiliar social situations
Flexible about how their time is used by others
Feels cramped by schedules
Flexible expectations about people and situations
Prefers to work with others
Initiates or accepts physical contact
Shares or enjoys listening to personal feelings, especially if positive

3

Animated facial expressions during speaking and listening
Shows more enthusiasm than the average person
Friendly handshake
More likely to give nonverbal feedback
Responsive to dreams, visions, and concepts

SELF-CONTAINED

2

Guarded
Keeps feelings private: shares only on a "need-to-know basis"
Makes most decisions based on evidence (objective)
Focuses conversation on issues and tasks; stays on subject
More formal and proper
Goes with the agenda
Fact-oriented
Takes time to get to know in business or unfamiliar social situations
Approaches risk, decisions, or change slowly and cautiously

1

Disciplined about how their time is used by others
Prefers following an established schedule
Fixed expectations about people and situations
Prefers to work independently
Avoids or minimizes physical contact
More likely to be expressionless during speaking and listening
Shows less enthusiasm than the average person
Uses limited range of facial expressions during speaking and listening
Formal handshake
Less likely to give nonverbal feedback if given at all
Responsive to realities/actual experiences/facts

SELF-CONTAINED

Figure 2B.   Open and Self-Contained Behaviors

The Four Basic Behavioral Styles

When you combine directness and openness behaviors on a grid, the four quadrants represent the four basic behavioral styles (see Figure 2C). This combination creates four patterns or styles of behavior: Steady Relater, Interactive Socializer, Dominant Director, and Cautious Thinker, as shown in Figure 2D. Their behavior is summarized in Figure 2E.

Indirect and open people are called *Steady Relaters*. Steady Relaters like to maintain the status quo in their lives. They like their world just the way it is and are somewhat reluctant to make changes. If you propose a plan that requires major changes, they are likely to ask you to reconsider, or at least suggest a change that is not as radical.

If you're ever selling to a Steady Relater, recognize that major changes represent a threat to their established world, and your plan is going to generate tension. Be ready to reassure the Steady Relater that everything is under control.

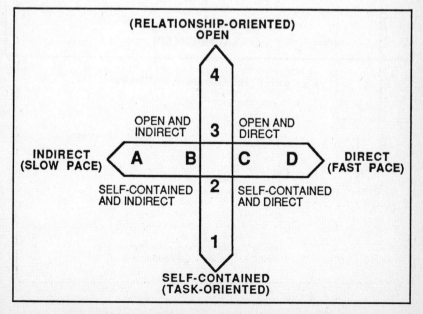

Figure 2C.   Combining the Openness and Directness Scales

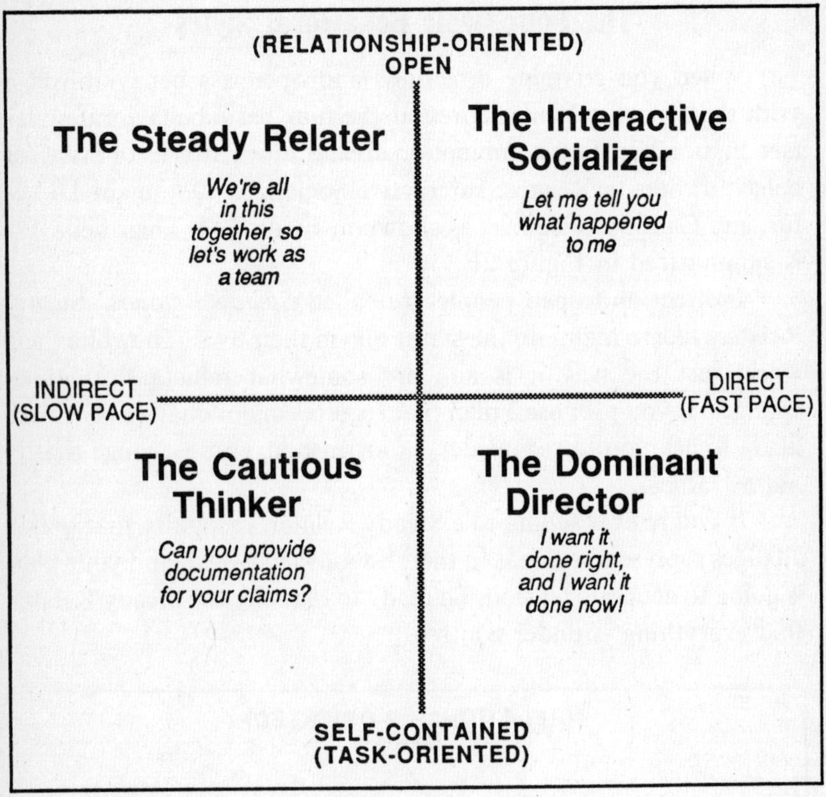

Figure 2D. The Four Behavioral Styles

	STEADY RELATER	CAUTIOUS THINKER	DOMINANT DIRECTOR	INTERACTIVE SOCIALIZER
BEHAVIOR PATTERN	Open/Indirect	Self-Contained/ Indirect	Self-Contained/ Direct	Open/Direct
APPEARANCE:	• Casual • Conforming	• Formal • Conservative	• Businesslike • Functional	• Fashionable • Stylish
WORK-SPACE:	• Personal • Relaxed • Friendly • Informal	• Structured • Organized • Functional • Formal	• Busy • Formal • Efficient • Structured	• Stimulating • Personal • Cluttered • Friendly
PACE:	Slow/Easy	Slow/ Systematic	Fast/Decisive	Fast/ Spontaneous
PRIORITY:	Maintaining relationships	The task: the process	The task: the results	Relationships Interacting
FEARS:	Confrontation	Embarrassment	Loss of control	Loss of prestige
UNDER TENSION WILL:	Submit/ Acquiesce	Withdraw/ Avoid	Dictate/Assert	Attack/ Be sarcastic
SEEKS:	Attention	Accuracy	Productivity	Recognition
NEEDS TO KNOW (BENEFITS)	• How it will affect his or her personal circum- stances	• How to justify the purchase logically • How it works	• What it does • By when • What it costs	• How it enhances his or her status • Who else uses it
GAINS SECURITY BY:	Close relationships	Preparation	Control	Flexibility
WANTS TO MAINTAIN:	Relationships	Credibility	Success	Status
SUPPORT HIS OR HER:	Feelings	Thoughts	Goals	Ideas
ACHIEVES ACCEPTANCE BY:	• Conformity • Loyalty	• Correctness • Thoroughness	• Leadership • Competition	• Playfulness • Being Entertaining
LIKES YOU TO BE:	Pleasant	Precise	Practical	Stimulating
WANTS TO BE:	Liked	Correct	In charge	Admired
IRRITATED BY:	• Insensitivity • Impatience	• Surprises • Unpredictability	• Inefficiency • Indecision	• Inflexibility • Routine
MEASURES PERSONAL WORTH BY:	• Compatibility with others • Depth of relationships	• Precision • Accuracy • Activity	• Results • Track record • Measurable progress	• Acknowledgment • Recognition • Applause • Compliments
DECISIONS ARE:	Considered	Deliberate	Definite	Spontaneous

Figure 2E. A Summary of Behavioral Styles

Cautious Thinkers are also indirect people. Like Steady Relaters, they tend to move slowly. But Cautious Thinkers are self-contained; they focus first on the task.

If you're selling to a Cautious Thinker, go slowly and focus on the business at hand. Cover the details, document your claims, go through each of the steps along the way. Don't skip anything. When you approach a Cautious Thinker, start by giving him or her an outline of your agenda. Explain it and then stick to it. Because if you get off the agenda, the Cautious Thinker will notice.

On the other side of the grid, we find the Dominant Director and the Interactive Socializer. *Dominant Directors* are self-contained, meaning task oriented, direct, fast moving. They don't mind taking a risk, because they want forward motion. They want progress and achievement more than anything else. Think of the Director on a movie set, or the Director on the Board of Directors. These people like to run things, they want to make their own decisions.

When you're selling to Dominant Directors, they don't want you to say "Here's what you should do." They want you to say "Here are your options. What do you think?" Remember, they need to make the decisions. Same outcome, different process.

Interactive Socializers are direct. They move quickly, but they are open; they focus on the relationship. They are playful and spontaneous. No matter what the situation, they've got a one-liner to slip in somewhere. Interactive Socializers love variety, hate routine. They can't stand to follow the same schedule every day.

When you're selling to Interactive Socializers, be stimulating. Spend your time showing the highlights and giving the big picture. Don't focus on the little details. It's good to have the details ready in case they want them but don't walk them through every step unless they ask. Otherwise, you're liable to lose your audience.

The more we know about the four personality types, the better able we are to sell to them. We know how to approach them, how to deal with them, how to manage them, and how to be successful with them.

Deal with people the way they want to be dealt with, not just the way you want to be dealt with.

Responding to Different Behavioral Styles

Now that you know the basics, let's focus on understanding each type in more detail.

The choices we make in life give people clues about our personality. Let's look at the choices a Steady Relater is likely to make. What type of job is the Steady Relater drawn toward? The helping professions—personnel, education, medicine, counseling, human resource development, religious vocations. These professions allow the Steady Relater to focus on relationships, express the openness pattern, and to take the slow, easy pace, the indirect pattern.

What type of job would the Cautious Thinker seek? Anything that has to do with the technical aspect of a particular field. Research, accounting, science. Cautious Thinkers are the technicians of the world and are largely drawn toward the exact sciences. Their preoccupation with detail would drive an Interactive Socializer nuts.

What about the Interactive Socializers? They choose public relations, performing arts, selling, advertising, professional speaking, anything that puts them in the spotlight. They need to be where the action is.

A Dominant Director is strong, forceful, outgoing, and competitive, and needs to be in control. What type of jobs do Dominant Directors seek? Jobs that let them be in charge. Managers, physicians, sales managers, drill sergeants, no matter what they're doing, they'll run the job like a command post.

Regardless of what product or service you're selling, when you call on someone, he or she will relate to you in a very predictable pattern consistent with personality type. The more you can tune in to a potential buyers' way of thinking and making choices, the more likely you will be to generate sales.

A person's behavior isn't always the same. Every personality includes Steady Relater, Cautious Thinker, Interactive Socializer, and Dominant Director traits. The behavior you see at any given time tells you what that person's needs are at that moment.

By behaving in a certain way, a potential buyer sends a message that says, "This is the way I prefer to be dealt with now." This can be confusing if you know a person is, for example, an Interactive Socializer, but the day you call on him you are seeing Dominant Director behavior. Which should you respond to? The Dominant Director behavior. Always respond to what you are seeing at that moment.

> *The behavior you see tells you how a person wants to be sold to at that moment.*

If you see Dominant Director behavior in a potential client, the first thing you want to do is get to the point. Show the client where you're going with your presentation, hit the high points, have documentation on hand (but don't walk through every step), and then show what the options are. Put the decision in the Dominant Director's hands. The Dominant Director wants to save time and move quickly.

If you encounter Interactive Socializer behavior, recognize that this person wants to talk. Start the conversation by asking questions so he or she can share information with you. The Interactive Socializer wants you to paint the big picture, show the exciting parts of that picture. Have the details if you're asked, but don't dwell on them. Then quickly get to the conclusion. This is the best way to sell to an Interactive Socializer.

If you're selling to a Cautious Thinker, be prepared to walk carefully through each step. Focus on accuracy, and don't rush into your conclusion. The Cautious Thinker wants to fully understand each detail along the way. Stick to your agenda. Be logical, precise, and accurate.

The Steady Relater is easy going, yet cautious about making quick decisions. Focus on developing a relationship. This personality type needs to feel comfortable with you before anything can happen. The Steady Relater needs to be able to trust you. Take your time, put him or her at ease, and answer all questions fully. Don't ever try to hedge on an answer with a Steady Relater, because Steady Relaters are naturally suspicious anyway.

Behavioral Flexibility

The underlying needs for each of the four personality types are quite basic. The Dominant Director's need is to get the job done; the Interactive Socializer wants to be noticed; the Cautious Thinker is concerned about accuracy; and the Steady Relater wants to maintain good relationships.

In order to relate to those underlying needs, you need to develop *behavioral flexibility*—the ability to adapt your own behavior appropriately to meet the needs of the person you're dealing with. This is *not* manipulation. You are not trying to change the other person; you are simply adapting your natural personality to meet the needs and comfort zone of the customer. The more you can develop flexibility in your own behavior, the more you can diminish the differences between you and the other person.

What this all boils down to is learning to practice not the Golden Rule, but the *Platinum Rule:*

"Do unto others as they would like to be done unto."

In other words, learn to treat people the way they want to be treated. Learn to sell to people the way they want to be sold to. Learn to adapt and adjust your own behavior, your timing, your information, your presentation, even the way you ask for the order so that your behavior is appropriate for the person you are dealing with (see Figure 2F).

Because when you modify your behavior and allow that person to remain in his or her own comfort zone, tension will be reduced.

When tension goes down, cooperation goes up. When cooperation goes up, guess what else goes up? That's right, *sales!*

Figures 2G, 2H, 2I, and 2J summarizes sales strategies for each of the behavioral types. Figure 2K provides a Relationship Action Plan you can use to plan your strategy for a particular client.

More information on *Relationship Strategies* is provided in the "Additional Resources" section starting on page 121.

YOUR STYLE

	STEADY RELATER	CAUTIOUS THINKER	DOMINANT DIRECTOR	INTERACTIVE SOCIALIZER
RELATER	• No change in openness or directness • Limit time spent in personal talk • Be responsible for initiating action • Establish deadlines and schedules	• Directness: no change • Openness: increase	• Directness: decrease • Openness: increase	• Directness: decrease • Openness: no change
	• General Strategies: support the client's feelings; show personal interest; accurately spell out objectives; when you disagree, discuss personal opinions and feelings; move along in an informal, slow manner; show that you are "actively" listening; provide guarantees that actions or decisions will involve a minimum of risk; offer personal assurances that you stand behind decisions. • To Motivate; show how it will strengthen the client's position with others.			
THINKER	• Directness: no change • Openness: decrease	• No change in openness or directness • Take control of direction of process; let customer control decisions or destiny • Accept less than perfection	• Directness: decrease • Openness: no change	• Directness: decrease • Openness: decrease
	• General Strategies: support the client's organized thoughtful approach; demonstrate through actions rather than words; give time to verify your words and actions; follow up personal contacts with a letter; provide solid, tangible, factual evidence that what you say is accurate; be systematic, exact, organized and prepared; list advantages and disadvantages of proposed plan. • To Motivate; appeal to the client's need to be accurate and logical; provide guarantees that actions can't backfire; avoid gimmicks.			

Figure 2F. Practicing Behavioral Flexibility (continued)

YOUR STYLE

	STEADY RELATER	CAUTIOUS THINKER	DOMINANT DIRECTOR	INTERACTIVE SOCIALIZER
DOMINANT DIRECTOR	• Directness: increase • Openness: decrease	• Directness: increase • Openness: no change	• No change in openness or directness • Remain receptive; don't impose your view • Let customer feel in control	• Directness: no change • Openness: decrease
	• General Strategies: support the client's goals and objectives; keep your relationship businesslike; if you disagree, argue facts, not personal feelings; give recognition to ideas, not the person; be precise, efficient, well organized; to influence decisions, provide alternatives and probabilities of their success. • To Motivate: provide options; clearly describe probabilities of success in achieving the Director's goals.			
INTERACTIVE SOCIALIZER	• Directness: Increase • Openness: no change	• Directness: increase • Openness: increase	• Directness: no change • Openness: increase	• No change in openness or directness • Exercise discipline — establish an agenda • Structure relationship by note-taking, verification, follow-up • Summarize agreements in writing
	• General Strategies: support the client's ideas and dreams; don't argue; don't hurry the discussion; nail down details verbally or in writing; be entertaining and fast moving; use testimonials to positively affect decisions. • To Motivate: offer incentives and testimonials.			

Figure 2F.   Practicing Behavioral Flexibility

Strengths

The strength of an Interactive Socializer lies in his or her enthusiasm and exciting, playful nature. Interactive Socializers quickly win people over and get others caught up in their drive to accomplish a task. They are fun to be with and can adapt easily to a changing situation. They always have something to say regardless of what the topic may be, and they usually say it in an interesting way.

Weaknesses

The Interactive Socializer's weaknesses result from an extension of their strengths. They sometimes come on too strong and are seen as being artificial or "put on." Sometimes their playfulness and spontaneity is regarded as a lack of seriousness or as unpredictability. They are not good detail people in that they are easily bored by anything that tends to be monotonous or has to be done alone.

General Strategies

Support opinions, ideas, and dreams.

Don't hurry the discussion.

Try not to argue.

Agree on the specifics of any agreement.

Summarize in writing what you both agreed upon.

Be entertaining and fast moving.

Use testimonials to positively affect decisions.

When Selling to Them

PLAN to be stimulating and interested in them. Allow them time to talk.

MEET them boldly; don't be shy. Introduce yourself first. Bring up new topics openly.

STUDY their dreams and goals as well as their other needs.

PROPOSE your solution with stories or illustrations that relate to them and their goals.

CONFIRM the details in writing. Be clear and direct.

ASSURE that they fully understand what they have bought and can demonstrate their ability to use it properly.

When Managing Them

TO MOTIVATE — offer them incentives and testimonials. They love to get "special deals."

TO COMPLIMENT — pay direct compliments to them as individuals.

TO COUNSEL — allow them plenty of opportunity to talk about things that are bothering them. Listen for the facts and the feelings. Probe and direct with questions. Many times Socializers merely need to "get something off their chest" and talking itself can solve the problem.

TO CORRECT — specify exactly what the problem happens to be and what appropriate behavior is required to eliminate the problem. Be sure you confirm in writing the agreed-upon behavior or changes.

TO DELEGATE — make sure you get clear agreement and establish check points so that there is not a long period of time between progress reports.

Above All Be: Interested in them.

Figure 2G.   Relationship Strategies for the Interactive Socializer

Strengths

The strengths of a Dominant Director are directness and ability to get the job done quickly. The Dominant Director is blunt and quite assertive and therefore gets fast results. Dominant Directors can generalize from details rather fast and see the big picture and the bottom line.

Weaknesses

The weaknesses of the Dominant Director grow out of the strengths, in that they can appear abrasive, insensitive to other people, and not concerned about details.

General Strategies

Support their goals and objectives.

Keep your relationship businesslike.

If you disagree, argue facts, not personal feelings.

Give recognition to ideas — not the person.

To influence decisions, provide alternate actions and probabilities of their success.

Be precise, efficient, time disciplined and well organized.

When Selling to Them

PLAN to be prepared and organized, fast paced, and to the point.

MEET them in such a way that you get to the point quickly, keeping things professional and businesslike.

STUDY their goals and objectives, what they want to accomplish, what is happening now, and how they would like to see it changed.

PROPOSE solutions with clearly defined consequences and rewards that relate specifically to the Dominant Director's goals.

CONFIRM by providing two to three options, and let them make the decision.

ASSURE them that their time will not be wasted. After the sale confirm that the proposals you suggested did in fact provide the bottom line results expected.

When Managing Them

TO MOTIVATE—provide them with options and clearly describe the probabilities of success in achieving their goals. Dominant Directors like to be winners.

TO COMPLIMENT—compliment what they have accomplished rather than complimenting them as a person.

TO COUNSEL—stick to the facts. Draw them out by talking about the desired results and discussing their concerns. Remember, they are much more task oriented than relationship oriented so they'll focus on things more than feelings.

TO CORRECT—describe what results were desired. Show them the gap between actual and desired. Suggest clearly the improvement that is needed and establish a time when they will get back to you. Don't hover over them when they are working on a task.

TO DELEGATE—give them the bottom line and then get out of their way, but so that they can be more efficient, give them parameters and guidelines to go by.

ABOVE ALL BE: PRACTICAL & EFFICIENT.

Figure 2H.   Relationship Strategies for the Dominant Director

Strengths

Cautious Thinkers tend to be precise, efficient, and well organized. They are task oriented and will persevere on what might otherwise be considered a boring task.

Weaknesses

Their weaknesses come from an extension of their strengths, in that they are often seen as too task oriented and too cool and impersonal. They are suspected of not being concerned about feelings because they place so much emphasis on facts. They may be perceived to be nitpickers who are such perfectionists that they can't be effective.

General Strategies

Support their organized, thoughtful approach.

Demonstrate through actions rather than words.

Be systematic, exact, organized, and prepared.

List advantages and disadvantages of any plan you propose.

Give them time to verify your words and actions.

Follow up your personal contacts with a letter.

Provide solid, tangible, factual evidence that what you say is true and accurate.

Do not rush the decision-making process.

Provide guarantees that actions can't backfire.

Avoid gimmicks.

When Selling to Them

PLAN to be well prepared and equipped to answer all their questions.

MEET them cordially but get quickly to the task.

STUDY the situation in a practical, logical manner. Ask lots of questions and make sure your questions show a clear direction. The better your questions fit into the overall scheme of things, the more likely they are to give you the appropriate answers.

PROPOSE logical solutions to their problems. Document the how and the why, and show how your proposition is the logical thing to do.

CONFIRM as a matter of course. Don't push; give them time to think. Offer documentation.

ASSURE them through adequate service and follow-through. Be complete.

When Managing Them

TO MOTIVATE — appeal to their need to be accurate and to their logical approach to things.

TO COMPLIMENT — compliment their efficiency and their efficient thinking processes; for example, "I like the way you think."

TO COUNSEL — describe the process that you will follow and outline how that process will produce the results they seek. Ask questions to help them give you the right information.

TO CORRECT — specify the exact behavior that is indicated and outline how you would like to see it changed. Establish check points and times.

TO DELEGATE — take time to answer all their questions about structure and guidance. The more they understand the details, the more likely they will be to complete the task properly. Be sure to establish target times and deadlines.

Above All Be: Thorough and well prepared.

Figure 2I.   Relationship Strategies for the Cautious Thinker

Strengths

The strengths of the Steady Relater are warmth and the ability to build meaningful relationships with others. They are loyal and compliant. They are excellent team workers, willing to conform.

Weaknesses

Their weaknesses grow out of an extension of their strengths in that some people see them as too concerned about relationships to do an adequate job of completing the task. Dominant Directors perceive them to be slow and ineffective. They are often so sensitive to the feelings and needs of others that they are unduly influenced by them.

General Strategies

Support their feelings.

Show personal interest.

Accurately spell out objectives.

When you disagree, discuss personal opinions and feelings.

Move along in an informal, slow manner.

Show that you are "actively" listening.

Provide guarantees that any actions will involve a minimum of risk.

Offer personal assurances that you will stand behind any decisions.

When Selling to Them

PLAN to get to know them personally. Be likable and nonthreatening, professional but friendly.

MEET them by developing trust, friendship, and credibility. Go at a slow pace.

STUDY their feelings and emotional needs as well as their technical and business needs. Take time to get them to spell out what is really important to them.

PROPOSE by getting them involved. Show the human side of your proposal. Show how it affects them and their relationships with others.

CONFIRM without pushing or rushing them. Provide personal assurances and guarantees wherever you can.

ASSURE by being consistent and regular in your communication. Give them the nurturing and reassurance that you would give someone who has highly concerned about the purchase they had just made.

When Managing Them

TO MOTIVATE — show them how it will benefit their relationships and strength their position with others.

TO COMPLIMENT — compliment the way they are regarded by other people, their relationship skills, their ability to get along with others.

TO COUNSEL — Allow plenty of time to explore their feelings and to understand the emotional side of the situation as well as the factual side. They tend to keep many of their feelings to themselves by stating tentatively what they mean. They are trying to express their feelings, but in an indirect way. Therefore, you'll need to draw them out through specific questioning and reflective listening techniques; for example, "This is what I heard you say . . . Is that what you meant?" Be sure to create a nonthreatening environment for them. Don't push or make them feel that they are getting the third degree.

TO CORRECT — reassure them that what you are seeking to correct is the behavior only. Don't blame or judge the person, but rather keep things focused on the behavior and it's appropriateness. Relaters tend to take everything personally; so you'll need to be extra cautious in the way you make your comments.

TO DELEGATE — appeal to them personally and also appeal to their loyalty. Give them the task, state the deadlines that need to be met, and explain why it's important to do it in that specific way.

Above All Be: Nonthreatening and sincere.

Figure 2J.   Relationship Strategies for the Steady Relater

Write the name and title of an individual with whom you would like your personal and professional interaction to be as effective as possible.

_____   _____
Name of Key Contact or Decision-Maker   Title

1. His or her general appearance is:

   ☐ Conservative and businesslike   ☐ Stylish or sporty
   ☐ Functional and authoritative   ☐ Pleasant and friendly

2. The theme that is most noticeable in his or her workspace is:

   ☐ Relaxed and casual   ☐ Strictly businesslike and functional
   ☐ Formal and efficient   ☐ Stylish and open

3. The style of his or her written correspondence is:

   ☐ Detailed and precise   ☐ Short and to the point
   ☐ Warm and friendly   ☐ Informal and dramatic

4. On the telephone he or she is:

   ☐ Strictly businesslike and brief   ☐ Short and to the point
   ☐ Playful and conversational   ☐ Warm and pleasant

5. In leisure pursuits, he or she is:

   ☐ Competitive and aggressive   ☐ Structured and sticks to the rules
   ☐ Casual and nonassertive   ☐ Spontaneous and playful

6. Based on the preceeding information, as
   well as your personal observations, rank
   the person's behavior on each of these scales:

                  Open (O)

                     4

                     3   Indirect (I)   A   B   C   D   Direct (D)

                     2

                     1

          Self-Contained (S)

Figure 2K.   A Relationship Action Plan

7. Based on your answer to Question 6, on the figure below, mark and "X" at the point that represents his/her position on this grid:

$$
\begin{array}{c}
\text{(O)} \\
4 \\
3 \\
\text{(I)} \quad \text{A} \quad \text{B} \quad \text{C} \quad \text{D} \quad \text{(D)} \\
2 \\
1 \\
\text{(S)}
\end{array}
$$

8. Your own behavioral style is: _____
   Mark your position on the above grid with an "S".

9. The main difference between the two of you is in the area of:

   ☐ Openness   ☐ Directness   ☐ Both

10. When you are with him or her, you will need to:

    ☐ Increase Directness   ☐ Increase Openness
    ☐ Reduce Directness   ☐ Reduce Openness

11. In dealing with this person, which type of atmosphere would you attempt to establish? (Check one.)

    ☐ Exciting, flexible, entertaining   ☐ Secure, easy, informal
    ☐ Steady, precise, serious   ☐ Direct, organized, efficient

12. This person's preference regarding the use of time is to: (Check one.)

    ☐ Develop the relationship   ☐ Ensure accuracy
    ☐ Enjoy the interaction   ☐ Act efficiently and effectively

13. The most comfortable pace for this person is: (Check one.)   ☐ Fast   ☐ Slow

14. This person expects the following kinds of information from a salesperson: (Check one.)

    ☐ Documentation and explanations   ☐ Options, probabilities, and bottom-line
    ☐ Personal guarantees and reassurance   results
                                              ☐ Summaries and testimonials

15. To facilitate this person's decision making, specifically what will you do?

    _____

    _____

16. In order to make him or her comfortable in your presence, how will you modify your Open and Direct behaviors (decrease/increase/no change necessary):

    Increase/Decrease Openness   How? _____

    Increase/Decrease Directness How? _____

Figure 2K.   A Relationship Action Plan (continued)

Part Three

How to Have an Endless Flow of People to Sell

"Cathcart's Four Rules of Dominoes" will help you understand marketing and building a business in such a way that you have an endless flow of clients.

Wouldn't it be great to have an endless flow of customers? Of course it would. You can, if you learn how to keep the sales pipeline full. "Cathcart's Four Rules Of Dominoes" will help you understand marketing and building a business in such a way that you have an endless flow of clients.

Rule #1 — You must have dominoes. If you're going to build a business and you want to line up your prospects one after another, first you must have something to line up. You've got to have prospects.

Rule #2 — You've got to line them up correctly. If you line them up properly, they'll all fall down quite nicely, thank you. But if you line them up incorrectly, you're not going to make any progress, because they won't fall against each other. What this means is that you've got to do your marketing and prospecting in such a way that one sale naturally leads to another.

Rule #3 — You've got to push the first domino in the right direction. When you make the first call, do it in such a way that it leads you right into another call, and another call. Make sure you take each contact very seriously. Be professional, and service the client after the sale is confirmed. Most important, let each client know that you want to specialize in that particular marketplace, that you want to understand that industry so you can be of better service, and that you want to meet even more people in that field of business.

Rule #4 — When you knock over the first domino, be ready for the rest of them to fall. They are going to fall, and if you're not ready for a lot of sales opportunities, then you're going to miss some of those opportunities and potentially spoil the marketplace.

Let's review the basics Marketing 101, just to refresh our memories. *Marketing is not selling*. Marketing is generating a *desire* for your product or service. Selling is converting that desire into *transactions*. Service is converting those transactions into *satisfied clients*.

Great Marketing + Poor Sales = Poverty

No matter how much demand there is, if you're not converting that demand into transactions, you're not going to have much success.

Great Sales + Poor Marketing = Burnout

Trying to sell without marketing makes for hard work. Each day selling is as hard as it was the day before, because nobody is helping. It's all on your shoulders every day.

Great Marketing + Great Sales + Poor Service = Surprises

A dissatisfied client will come back to haunt you every time. Usually this happens when you least expect it, when you're least prepared, and when it's most embarrassing for you.

Great Service + Poor Marketing + Poor Sales = Loneliness

If you provide great service but you haven't generated marketing and sales for your product you're going to suffer from the "Maytag Syndrome," sitting around wishing you had somebody to serve. You need all three, marketing, sales, and service, to be truly successful.

What Is a Market?

Let's identify exactly what a market is. This is important, because the more clearly you can identify a particular market, the more you can control the growth of your business over the years.

A *market* is a group of people who have enough in common that you can establish a reputation among them. If you can build a reputation among a group of people, then each sales call becomes easier. The goal of marketing is to give you a large number of people who are willing to see you. The more you can create a demand for your product or service, the more you can build a reputation for yourself.

> *Marketing makes selling easier. Marketing brings the stress level down, the cooperation level up.*

Your markets will fall into two general categories: *natural* markets and *chosen* markets. A *natural market* is one that you've already made inroads to. You don't have to start at square one and build a lot of connections. Natural markets come out of existing relationships and leads that have grown out of previous contacts and experience.

A *chosen market* is one that you decide to go after. You see an opportunity, gather information, establish contacts, and develop and cultivate this chosen market.

To help you define your natural market, think of friends you have who know your capabilities and would make good potential clients. For example, list old school friends, neighbors, family friends, friends you've met through your spouse or children, friends you know through hobbies, church, social clubs, or community activities. What about friends and associates you know through past employment and people you do business with today? Any number of these people could possibly benefit from having your product or service. This natural market is an excellent source of potential clients. Friends who know your capabilities and degree of professionalism can provide the beginning of a friendship "tree" of potential clients. List two friends in each of the categories shown in Figure 3A. As you contact each of these potential clients, he or she may be able to add two more names to make your tree grow.

Friendship Tree*

Evaluate the demographic characteristics of each friend to maximize your efficiency and not waste their time. Age, occupation, length of time known, how well known, how often seen, ability to provide referrals, and how easy it is to approach this person are some factors to consider.

TYPE OF FRIEND   **LIST TWO NAMES**

School friends: _____
_____

Neighbors: _____
_____

Known through spouse: _____
_____

Known through children: _____
_____

Known through hobbies: _____
_____

Known through church: _____
_____

Known through social clubs: _____
_____

Known through
community activities: _____
_____

Known through past employment: _____
_____

People you do business with: _____
_____

Others: _____
_____

Figure 3A. A Friendship Tree

*Thanks to Steve Curtis of Newport Beach, CA for this exercise.

From *The Business of Selling*, Alessandra & Cathcart, Prentice-Hall

A way to help develop your *chosen* market is to think of building a *reservoir* of potential clients. Think of the general flow of business as a giant ocean, a part of which you will channel into your own reservoir.

From within your reservoir, select individuals who would be good, qualified buyers for your product or service. Put these people into your *inventory* — a list of contacts who are willing and eager to see you whenever you are ready to initiate the meeting.

Add to your reservoir the names you accumulated from your natural market; list "opportunity prospects," people you have observed who may need your services; list the names of your *key targeted markets*, those specific markets you will go after.

For each of the groups in your reservoir, develop a *market profile* (see Figure 3B). In the market profile list the categories within that market. for example, under doctors you might list orthopedist, internist, general practitioner, and so on.

Next list some of the specifics relevant to those categories. For example, how many meetings they typically hold or attend each year, average annual income, or the products they buy within a year. Of course, the specifics will be different for each field of business you analyze.

Think carefully about what to list under each targeted market. Your result will be a reservoir you can draw from for the rest of your career. With well-planned target marketing, you never run out of people to see. You will never again be without prospects.

At this point, let me specify the difference between a *nest* and a *market*. A nest is a small group of people with something in common. For example, the residents of a new housing development. It is possible to saturate a nest in a limited time. A market, by contrast, is virtually bottomless. The reservoir keeps refilling.

Within your market profile, you have a list of names of key people you want to contact and a demographic profile of the marketplace. Add to that a list of associations or societies your targeted group may belong to and determine which publications they read. Be familiar with the major events they are likely to attend.

A MARKET PROFILE CONSISTS OF:
- A list of names of key people
- A demographic profile of the marketplace
- A list of associations and societies
- Publications they read
- Major events they attend
- Major categories within this market
- Psychographics (how they think)
- Common fears, likes, dislikes, goals
- Challenges they are facing
- Some of the catch words and jargon they use

Figure 3B. A Market Profile. The more fully you understand each market, the more you will be able to succeed in selling to them.

What are the *psychographics* of your targeted group? In other words, "How do these people think?" What are the schools of thought your group is likely to follow? Learn the jargon or terminology commonly used by your targeted market. Words mean different things to different groups. For example, *habit* means one thing in psychology, but something very different to the clergy. So be careful how you use terms and phrases.

Learn what the common likes and dislikes are for your group. Be familiar with their fears, their goals, and the challenges they face.

All of this will add to your understanding of each market. The more fully you understand each market, the more likely you are to succeed in selling to them.

Once you've developed your reservoir, and you've been adding to it each day or each week as you find new opportunities, it then becomes time to prepare each name in the reservoir to move into your inventory, to go from having a group of names to having some specific people to call on. There are a number of ways you can do that.

There are any number of ways to cultivate your target market. In fact, selling becomes harder than it needs to be if you don't follow this marketing concept. You can improve your business by increasing your *effort* or increasing your *effectiveness*. Increasing your effectiveness is probably the smarter of the two. There's no limit to how "smart" you can work, how effective you can be.

Among the techniques for market cultivation are:

Promotion — The form promotion takes depends on what field you're in. It can be having a booth at an industry convention or trade show, demonstrating your products or services at a mall or other public access area, undertaking a direct-mail promotion that may include some type of a response card, and more.

Publicity — Publicity is *free advertising*. Try to get the local paper to run an article about you, or see if you can appear as a guest on a TV show. This is publicity, and it is very helpful in getting your name out to the marketplace.

Advertising — Place ads in key publications that appeal to your target market. You may even want to hire an advertising or public relations firm to promote you.

Articles — Submit articles you have written about your product or service to key publications. Your by-line will give you appropriate, professional exposure and generate interest in you, your company, and your product or service.

Networking — Networking is a fancy term for talking to a lot of people, building relationships. You may want to start or join a "tip club," whose members meet informally and share leads. For example, if I know that you're in real estate, and I hear that my neighbor is planning to sell his house, I'll share that information, or lead, with you. The next time you hear of someone who needs my product or service, you'll share that lead with me.

Service clubs — When you join a service club, don't join with the attitude of exploiting the club for your own gain. Join because you truly like what that club does and what it stands for. It's perfectly okay, though, to introduce yourself and let the other members know what you do for a living.

Qualifying Your Prospects

When you move names from your reservoir into your inventory, you need to qualify your prospects through a five-way checklist. Good prospects need to meet the following criteria:

1. You need to have enough **information** about a person to make contact with him or her. A company name is not enough. You need an individual's name and title, address, and phone number.

2. The prospect must have a **probable need** that you can fill. If you don't suspect that he or she has such a need, then perhaps that person shouldn't be on your inventory list.

3. The prospect must have the **ability to buy**. You can't always know for sure, but you can get a good feel for ability to buy by studying the group and the market within which this prospect operates.

4. The prospect must have the **authority to make the buying decision**. If that person can't make buying decisions, you're prospecting the wrong person.

5. The prospect should have enough **awareness** of your field to understand and appreciate what you have to offer. It becomes wastefully time-consuming when you have to educate everyone from square one. Deal with people who are sophisticated enough about your field to at least partially understand how you can help them.

Once a prospect has passed the five-way qualification, you create a *prospective client card* and put that name into your inventory.

It's a good idea to cross-reference the cards by filing them both monthly and alphabetically. The monthly file tells you exactly whom to call on that month, and the alphabetical file allows you to find the card quickly.

To each card, assign a letter code: A, B, C, D, or E.

- An **A** prospect is someone who has high potential value and is easy to get in to see.

- A **B** prospect has high potential value, but is very difficult to get in to see.

- A **C** prospect is someone who has low potential value, but is easy to get in to see.

- A **D** prospect has low potential value and is very difficult to get in to see.

- A **E** is someone you're just not sure about yet. You need more information to qualify him or her correctly.

Devote most of your time to the A's and B's, because they are potentially the most lucrative. The C's are very tempting, but should be seen only when it will not take prime selling time away from the A's and B's.

A Review of the Marketing Process

Let's review the marketing process. We start with an ocean of people and, through target marketing, select certain names to be in the reservoir. By using the five-way qualifying checklist, we move selected names from the reservoir into the inventory. Through contacting prospects, the inventory is moved into the sales pipeline. And people move from the sales pipeline to the client pool through sales and service.

Contacting Potential Clients

There are many ways to contact people, either on your own or working with a sales staff, but I have found the following to be the most beneficial:

Telephone canvassing — Canvassing is making a lot of calls on moderately qualified buyers. The purpose is to further qualify each contact, to generate as much possible business in the least amount of time and at the least expense. The more qualified each contact is, the more likely you are to generate a sale.

There are many ways to handle telephone canvassing. For example, the "boiler room" set-up, with many phones in operation. This plan requires that each caller have a script to follow. You can generate a lot of contacts with this approach. But this is a "going-for-the-numbers" technique, and it does have its shortcomings. You have to be careful that your script doesn't sound "canned" or awkward and that the script is truly appropriate to the type of people being called.

Phone clinic — A phone clinic works very well for new salespeople. Have your sales staff meet once a week to discuss their telephone techniques. Following the meeting, have each person go into his or her office to make calls. After thirty minutes or so, have them gather in the meeting room again to share their experiences. They will learn from each other what works and what doesn't. After a few weeks of sharing through the clinic format, their sales will increase, and each call will prove more productive. Even after they have improved, it's a good idea to keep the clinic going occasionally for the feedback it offers each salesperson.

Introductory calls — An introductory call is a personal visit to someone who didn't suspect that you were coming, but it's far more professional than the old "cold call" approach. On an introductory call, you introduce yourself and your company, state the reason for the visit, and ask if it's convenient for them to talk for a moment. If it's appropriate to sell at that time, do so. If not, schedule an appointment for a later meeting. Be appropriate and professional — not aggressive — when making an introductory call.

Referrals and appointments — Referral prospecting is easier, because people give you names of and information about potential clients. You can ask questions of the person giving you the referral and establish whether the prospect is a qualified buyer even before your initial contact.

Letter followed by a call — This is a very good way of introducing yourself. Use the letter to make the introduction and the phone call to make the appointment or the sale. Whenever you contact someone by phone, know ahead of time whether they can buy your product or service over the phone. If not, use the phone call to sell the appointment, not the product. You then sell the product when you meet face to face.

This chapter has presented a lot of different ways to qualify the people in your inventory so that you can really benefit from your list of names. The goal is to help you create an endless flow of people who are willing and eager to see you.

Many of the specific techniques I have mentioned may already be in your kit of selling tools. Use the format of this chapter to help you re-examine the flow of people from ocean to reservoir to inventory to customer.

Part Four

Diagnosis — Finding Buyer Wants and Needs

A professional salesperson should diagnose the customer's needs and wants *before* telling them what they should buy.

In selling, as in medicine, prescription before diagnosis is malpractice.

When you walk into the office of any professional person, you hope to find someone who will take a specific interest in you, study your circumstances, analyze every detail, and then make the correct prescription for your particular situation. A professional salesperson should do the same thing — diagnose customers' needs and wants *before* telling them what they should buy.

> *In selling, as in medicine, prescription before diagnosis is malpractice.*

The more accurately you can diagnose the needs and wants of your customer, the more appropriately you can prescribe the right product or service, the right package, and the right prices for this particular individual.

Remember, people love to buy. They truly want to cooperate. And if you do your job right, they will make selling easy for you. All you need to do is help people overcome their natural resistance to buying. They want to be sure they're buying the right thing. If you take the time to diagnose their needs and wants, you'll be in a position to recommend the right product or service to meet their needs.

When you take the time to diagnose, you seem more professional, you encounter less resistance, you make sales that last longer, and you often make a larger sale than you might have made otherwise.

Identifying Buyer Wants and Needs

What is the difference between a *want* and a *need*, and which one is more important? For example, the customer may *want* a Hawaiian cruise, while his *need* is for an office computer. Which one he acts upon is dependent on how effectively you sell. If you're really doing your job right, you should be able to show the customer how he can get both, although maybe not at the same time.

Good selling meets real needs while also addressing wants. Meet their needs, yet acknowledge their wants in such a way that you show them how fulfillment of those wants will be possible. For example, you might point out how they'll save enough money on your product or service to later take the cruise they want.

In diagnosis the first rule is: *Know what to look for*. You can't help a buyer with his or her wants and needs if you don't know a buyer when you see one. To help you identify a potential buyer, I suggest you create a Buyer Profile, a checklist that you can use to identify the qualities, traits, or particular situations that are necessary for a person to be an ideal buyer for you. Not just any buyer, an *ideal* buyer. What would an ideal buyer for your product or service look like?

Some criteria you may wish to consider for your Buyer Profile are:

- The customer's ability to buy.

- The customer's desire to buy. Having money available isn't enough. The customer must have a desire to buy what your product delivers.

- The customer's need to buy.

- Can this person really use your product or service? If not, your chances of making a repeat sale are limited.

Think of those other criteria specific to your industry that you may wish to add to your Buyer Profile.

Identifying the Decision Maker

One key question to ask when you meet a potential buyer is "Who usually makes the buying decisions for your company?" You want to determine right away whether you are talking to the right person. If the person you are talking to responds with: "I screen the products and recommend the top three to the supervisor for a final decision," then you know you have to make two sales. One to the contact, and one to the supervisor. The contact will become your temporary sales representative, so you had better have that contact well trained by the time the decision maker gets involved.

There are a number of things you can do to prepare your contact to represent you and recommend your product or service to the final decision maker:

1. Outline the key points and summarize the main reasons why that company should buy from you.

2. Include enough copies of your sales material that each person who might be in on the discussion would have his or her own copy to read.

3. Highlight key points that make your product or service different from the competition, and put those points in writing.

> *If you don't take the time to prepare your contact to represent you, you reduce your chances of being recommended.*

If you are selling to a group, try to determine how buying decisions are typically made within that group. Watch carefully to see who defers to whom in making even the small decisions. The way they handle the little decisions may very well be the way they handle the large ones. Tailor your presentation to reach the key people.

Until you know the facts about how a potential buyer makes buying decisions, it's difficult for you to truly serve that customer. Here are some questions you'll need answers to:

- Where does the decision maker get his or her information?

- If there is more than one decision maker, in what sequence are decisions like this made?

- How are major decisions made in this firm?

- Who reports to whom? (To know in advance, check with a secretary and determine titles and reporting sequence.)

- Is there a break-off point where this person's decision-making authority ends? Example: for decisions above $1000 the supervisor must be consulted prior to buying.

- Does someone else do the screening of purchases before the buying decision is made?

- In the case of a committee, who will present your ideas to the group? And who has the most authority in that committee?

- In the case of an inquiry (they called you), did the person making the call really initiate the contact or was he or she asked to contact you by someone else?

- Who besides the decision maker influences the choices that are made?

- What does the buyer really want and need?

The Importance of Listening

To learn what you want to know, you may have to sharpen up your listening skills. Pay attention to what that buyer is communicating to you.

People don't care what you know until they know that you care.

The quickest way to show that you care is by listening. It requires a little effort on your part to be an effective listener. Listening is not just sitting back and hearing words roll by. It requires your active participation.

Listening is not just hearing, it's *wanting* to hear. It's a way to say to your customer, "Hey, I really care about you." Listening is hard for us to master because most of us were never taught how to listen. We're taught how to read, write, and speak, but we have never been taught how to listen. Learn to listen CAREfully.

C   Concentrate

A   Acknowledge

R   Restate

E   Empathize

Concentrate — Do what you can to remove both the internal and external distractions, so you can really concentrate on what your customer is saying. Often you will have no control over the internal moods, feelings, or preoccupations of that customer, but you do have some control over your own internal distractions. Focus all of your attention on this customer at this time.

To control external distractions, ask the customer if he or she minds if you turn off the TV, close the blinds, lower the radio, or move to more comfortable chairs.

Internal and external distractions can affect your own and your customer's ability to concentrate. Control the environment when you can, and compensate for it when you can't.

Acknowledge — Show your customer that you're listening. Even a gentle nod of your head is a good way to reinforce your customer's remarks. Acknowledging is vital to your success in sales. It's the one thing you can do in selling that will have more impact on the quality of the relationship with that client than any other skill you can employ. Imagine talking with someone who never responded to let you know you were getting through.

Restate — In your own words, restate what the customer has just said to you. This serves two purposes: It shows that you have been listening, and it gives you a chance to test the water to be sure that you heard correctly and that your presentation is on target.

Empathize — Let that client know you understand how he or she feels. The client needs to know that you truly understand the situation and that you can deal with it in an appropriate manner. To accomplish this, practice what I call the "Think as if you were the buyer" technique. Put yourself in the place of the buyer and ask yourself how you would feel if you were in his or her present set of circumstances.

To listen effectively, avoid displaying irritating listening habits. Read the following list of 23 listening habits* buyers find distinctly irritating. Identify those you are sometimes guilty of, so you can correct them.

1. He does all the talking; I go in with a problem and never get a chance to open my mouth.

2. She interrupts me when I talk.

3. He never looks at me when I talk. I'm not sure he's listening.

4. She continually toys with a pencil, paper or some other item while I'm talking; I wonder if she's listening.

5. His poker face keeps me guessing whether he understands me or is even listening to me.

6. She never smiles — I'm afraid to talk to her.

7. He changes what I say by putting words into my mouth that I didn't mean.

8. She puts me on the defensive when I ask a question.

9. Occasionally he asks a question about what I have just told him that shows he wasn't listening.

10. She argues with everything I say — even before I have a chance to finish my case.

*From Anthony Alessandra, Ph.D., La Jolla, CA.

11. Everything I say reminds him of an experience he's either had or heard of. I get frustrated when he interrupts, saying "That reminds me . . ."

12. When I am talking, she finishes sentences for me.

13. He acts as if he is just waiting for me to finish so he can interject something of his own.

14. All the time I'm talking, she's looking out the window.

15. He looks at me as if he is trying to stare me down.

16. She looks as if she's appraising me . . . I begin to wonder if I have a smudge on my face, a tear in my coat, etc.

17. He looks as if he is constantly thinking "No" or questioning the truthfulness or value of what I'm saying.

18. She overdoes showing she's following what I'm saying . . . too many nods of her head, or mm-hm's, and uh-huh's.

19. He sits too close to me.

20. She frequently looks at her watch or the clock while I am talking.

21. He is completely withdrawn and distant when I'm talking.

22. She acts as if she is doing me a favor in seeing me.

23. He acts as if he knows it all, frequently relating incidents in which he was the hero.

You'll never go wrong by practicing effective listening. When you listen and show that you care, it lowers tension, opens communication, builds cooperation, and increases sales.

Asking Questions

The other side of the communication is *questioning*. Don't ask just any questions, but questions that will help you to understand the needs, wants, and situation of your buyer. Show that you value your customer's time by making your questions productive and purposeful. In order to do that, develop a Questioning Plan for every call you make.

To develop your Questioning Plan, think of a funnel, broad at the top, narrow at the bottom. Start off with broad, nonthreatening questions. Questions that ask for general information about your buyer and his or her business. Make even these broad questions relevant to why you are calling on this person. Gradually become more specific. Here are some of the questions you'll need answers to:

- How will they use that?
- Who else is bidding?
- When will the decision be made?
- What other needs do they have?
- How could they benefit from having more than one?
- How long is their payment cycle?
- Why is this particular item so important to them?

If you build up slowly, the buyer will be more receptive to answering specific questions, because you have taken the time to build trust and cooperation.

There are four types of questions I have found to be the most beneficial in a sales situation:

Clarifying — Use clarifying questions to bring your information together to see if you're on target. For example, "Let me see, Mr.

Jones, if I understand you correctly . . ." Clarify your understanding of the information the buyer has given you.

Verifying — Use verifying questions to check your conclusions, data, or facts, to confirm an existing conclusion. "It sounds like you are planning to make the decision this week. Is that correct?"

Expanding — Seeking new information on a subject you are *already* discussing. "How else do you use these products?"

Directing — Changing the direction of the conversation and bringing up a new subject can move the buyer into scheduling or ordering and help you start to confirm the sale. "With that in mind, how can we begin to take action to avoid those problems next month?"

There are two *styles* of questions, each serving a different purpose. *Closed-ended* questions call for a specific response, usually a fact. For example, "How many employees work in your headquarters office?"

An *Open-ended* question usually begins with *who*, *what*, *when*, *where*, *why*, or *how*, and allows for varied responses. An open-ended question lets the buyer choose how he or she wants to respond. An open-ended question is a good way to let the buyer express how he or she feels about an issue. "How do you feel that this situation is affecting your profitability?" You can pick up valuable information not only by what is said, but by how it is said as well.

If you want selling to go well for you, design an appropriate Questioning Plan and have a purpose and direction to your questions. Good questions show that you care about that customer and that you have taken the time to be familiar enough with their business to ask meaningful, intelligent questions. Figure 4A provides guidelines for developing a Questioning Plan.

Practice developing sales questions by using these categories:

- Opening questions

- Questions to uncover decision-making authority

- Questions to discover needs

(Continued on page 64)

GUIDELINES FOR DEVELOPING A QUESTIONING PLAN

Plan your questions in advance so that you are sure to obtain the answers you need. Begin by listing the information you need and then develop questions which will uncover that information.

Begin with broad questions and progress to more specific ones.

Build on the buyer's previous responses when formulating your next questions.

Eliminate the use of jargon or technical terms which might confuse the buyer.

Ask questions which focus on one idea at a time.

Keep the questions short and simple.

Make the questions nonthreatening.

Give a reason for needing to know before you ask sensitive questions.

Ask questions which uncover desired benefits rather than focusing on features.

Uncover the ideal solutions. (If the world were perfect, what would you like this product to do for you?)

Figure 4A. Developing a Questioning Plan

- Questions to discover wants
- Questions to verify your conclusions or data
- Questions to clarify wants and needs
- Questions to expand the discussion further
- Questions to direct the discussion into new areas
- Questions to uncover unstated concerns or objections
- Questions to confirm the purchase
- Questions to verify that the buyer understands what he or she has bought

Keep your list of questions handy and review them prior to each sales interview.

To Summarize

The steps for successfully determining a potential buyer's wants and needs can be summarized as follows:

1. Know what a buyer looks like.

2. Find the decision maker

3. Know what information you need

4. Develop a questioning plan

5. Listen carefully

6. Follow your plan

Part Five

Prescription — Giving Winning Presentations

To be successful, a salesperson must be able to find and address the *dominant buying motive* of each client.

The question I am asked most often is, "How do I present my product or service so that the person wants to buy it?" I think this is a great question for a salesperson to be asking, because a good presentation is essential to your success.

> *A good presentation builds buyer confidence in both you and your product.*

When you think about how you are going to present your product or service, remember that every buyer has in his or her mind a scale. The scale contains two bowls: one bowl is *price* (what the buyer pays); the other bowl is *value* (what the buyer gets). Until value outweighs price in the buyer's mind, no sale will be made.

Don't overlook the importance of a good presentation. You may be well qualified and you may really care about the person you're dealing with. But that doesn't mean you'll get the sale. Many times the way you present yourself and your product or service seems more important to the buyer than your ability to deliver. Buyers want to be able to trust you and feel confident with you. More often than not, it's your *presentation* that establishes, or fails to establish, this confidence.

Think back to our discussion in Chapter 1 about traditional selling. The old style of selling relied on the sales pitch to get the sale. We know this just doesn't work anymore — a fancy sales pitch isn't enough to convince the customer to buy. You've got to be *we* oriented, not *me* oriented. Do a thorough job of planning before the meeting, and be ready, willing, and able to follow up the sale with service and satisfaction.

The presentation should not be an isolated event separate from the rest of the sales call. It should be an integral part of it. There shouldn't be an abrupt break when you obviously launch into a sales pitch. If the buyer senses that you are doing just that, it comes across as "canned" and artificial.

To show a buyer the value of your product or service, you first must determine what that buyer believes is valuable. Until you address the wants and needs of your buyer, it doesn't matter how great your product or service is. The buyer needs to know that you're offering something of value to him or her.

Every customer carries in his or her head the WIIFM question:

> *WIIFM = What's In It For Me?*

All buyers want to know what's in it for them. What will they be getting for their money? As we found out in Part 4, you can determine what is of value to the buyer by asking good questions and really listening to the answers. Focus on the wants, needs, and concerns of your buyer, not on the product.

The Presentation — A Dialogue

To be successful, a salesperson must be able to find and address the *dominant buying motive* of each client. The client may very well have more than one buying motive, but your job is to determine which one or two motives dominate, and to be ready to address them.

Let's look at some of the basic human wants:

Want To Gain	Want To Avoid
Comfort	Criticism
Money	Embarrassment
Time	Loss of property
Health	Trouble or unhappiness
Praise	Missing opportunities
Acceptance	Loss of respect
Control	Extra effort
Respect	Pain and confusion

If you can show the buyer how to achieve his or her goals and avoid problems, you'll be successful, because you'll be on target with the buying motives of that individual.

A sales presentation should be a dialogue, not a long-winded monologue. People like to feel involved, and they will support what they've helped create. Build your presentation so the buyer can participate. Yo can be sure that this is far more effective than just announcing the benefits of your product one after another. Allow the buyer to comment or ask a question.

There are many ways you can make your presentation, but the ultimate success of that presentation depends on two factors: the *medium* and the *message*.

The *medium* is how you present yourself — the package your message comes in. This includes how you dress and speak and how your material looks upon presentation. The medium is the outside package, and it's the first thing the buyer sees.

The *message* is the *thoughts* you want to convey — What your product or service will do for the buyer. The message is what's inside the presentation package.

Presentation Styles

Let's look at some presentation styles you may wish to employ:

Direct Mail — Sending out a piece of mail results in one-way communication. You have control over the content of your mail piece, but you have no control over how it is interpreted or utilized. One of the strengths of direct mail is its ability to reach a large market all at once.

Written Proposal — A written proposal is a professional-looking introduction, but it doesn't allow you to hear the customer's feedback. Unless you are there to go through it with the buyer, it may not be read the way you would like it to be read.

Recorded Presentation — An audio or video recording is an excellent way to impart a lot of information in a short time. But if your recording is played under the wrong circumstances, if distractions compete for the viewers' attention, it may not have the impact you had hoped for. Also, if you can't control who will see or hear the recording, it may be played for people who are not the key decision makers, and, this will also reduce its impact as a sales tool.

Telephone Calls — The telephone call is probably the most valuable sales tool we have. It's two-way communication, quick and easy to use. The telephone is an excellent way to make an introductory call and set up an appointment for a presentation. However, customers can't see you over the telephone, so they have to guess what you look like. Remember, people can tell if you're smiling just by hearing your voice. So when you call, make sure you have a positive attitude toward your work. Don't make the call until you do. Using the phone to make an appointment can save you a great deal of travel money, because that way, when you do travel, it won't be a wasted effort.

Group Presentations — You can use the group presentation to reach several people at once. While you're there, determine who the actual decision maker is and deal with that person one-on-one when asking for the sale. People who have learned how to speak in front of a group are respected and admired. They appear confident and in control of the situation. If you're good at public speaking, take advantage of that acquired skill and give group presentations. It increases your chances of making sales.

Face-to-Face Calls — You really have all of the benefits of one-to-one contact going for you in a face-to-face call, but this can be a very expensive way to sell. Consider your cost for calling on each potential buyer face to face. This is your chance to make the most of your time with that buyer. Make it a pleasing experience, use eye contact, and interact with what the client says. Face to face calls are excellent for building relationships and confirming the sale.

Study the six types of presentations just described and develop the best combination to suit your product, your market, and your own personal feelings about how you like to sell. Whenever possible, choose the style of presentation with the maximum human contact. The more interactive it is, the better the results will be.

Most salespersons should use the mail to deliver information and generate responses. The written proposal works best if you can deliver it in person and walk the buyer through the material. Recordings work well to enhance an in-person presentation and allow the buyer to see what you have been describing. Unless your product or service can be easily sold over the telephone, use the phone only to schedule appointments. Do your selling in person. Speeches are best followed-up with one-on-one contact, and face-to-face calls are primarily used to confirm the sale.

Using a Sales Planning Guide

No matter which type of presentation you choose, the first steps in selling should always be planning and preparation. Being well organized and prepared helps you avoid embarrassment, gives you more control, saves time, increases your confidence, and increases your sales.

Use a Sales Planning Guide (Figure 5A) as a checklist to gather the right information and structure your material so that you're always selling confidently. The Sales Planning Guide in Figure 5A can serve as a general guideline for formulating your own, specific to your particular industry.

Preparing a Good Presentation

When you have completed your sales guideline for your prospective client, you are ready to prepare your presentation. A good presentation should be thorough — it should cover all the bases and key

SALES PLANNING GUIDE *

Company _____ Type of business _____

Location _____ Phone _____ Date _____

Key contact _____ Title _____

Who is the decision maker? _____

Current situation: _____

Goals and objectives? _____

Potential problem(s) or need(s):

_____

What objectives should I seek to accomplish with this account?

Next call:

Overall:

_____

If the key contact is not the decision maker, how can he or she influence the objective(s) I am trying to achieve?

_____

What questions can I ask to uncover, clarify, or amplify prospect problems, needs, or goals?

_____

What decision-making criteria are important to this prospect?

_____

FOR VALUE UNITS

Possible benefits prospect is seeking:	Features I offer that provide those benefits:	Possible proof materials (letters, testimonials) to be used if necessary:

How can I be of more benefit to this prospect than anyone else who has called on him or her?

_____

Prospect's possible concerns & questions	Potential answers
1. _____	1. _____
2. _____	2. _____
3. _____	3. _____

Based on my objective(s), what specific commitment will I ask this prospect to make?

Why should the prospect want to make this commitment?

_____

By what criteria will the prospect judge whether or not my product, service, or company was a satisfactory solution to his problem or need?

Figure 5A. Example Sales Planning Guide

*From *The Business of Selling*, Alessandra & Cathcart, Prentice-Hall

points. Mention features and benefits that are missing in the competitor's line. Show how your product or service can better meet the client's needs and wants.

> *A good presentation should stay clear of jargon and technical terms the client doesn't understand.*

Remember, your objective is to communicate and make a sale, not to impress the buyer with your knowledge of esoteric terms and phrases. Seldom is the buyer impressed. In fact, customers are more likely to do business with the salesperson who understands *their* needs and communicates in *their* language.

The presentation should build confidence in you, your product or service, and your company. You can build this confidence by letting the buyer participate in the presentation. Remember, people tend to support what they've helped create. Structure your presentation in the *buyer's* order of importance; yet be flexible enough so that if you're interrupted you can restate your main points and continue smoothly.

Figure 5B summarizes the characteristics of a good presentation.

Three Types of Presentations

There are three major types of presentations in selling, and each has its benefits and its drawbacks. The three types are *memorized*, *outlined*, and *prescriptive*.

Memorized — The memorized presentation gives you control of the conversation and often works well to help a beginning salesperson stay on track. It works well on the telephone because it helps you get right to the point of why you called. Quality is consistent, because your presentation always includes the same material. One of the drawbacks of this approach is that a memorized presentation is really

A GOOD PRESENTATION SHOULD BE:

Thorough — cover all the bases and key points.

A competition eliminator.

Clear of jargon and technical terms.

A confidence builder.

Presented in the buyer's language.

AND IT SHOULD:

Show how your features deliver the right benefits.

Be structured in the buyer's order of importance.

Keep the buyer involved.

Reinforce all positive statements made by the buyer.

Present one value unit at a time.

Be flexible enough that if interrupted you can restate your main
    points and continue smoothly.

Figure 5B.   Essentials for a Good Presentation

a "canned" speech, and unless carefully delivered, can come across
as insincere or awkward.

Outlined — Making an outlined presentation is more like giving
a speech on a subject you are very comfortable with. The outline
reminds you of the key points you want to cover, but it is not a
word-for-word script. To use an outlined presentation, a salesperson
must be more competent and sure of his or her material. This approach
would be a good choice for a group presentation in which you want
to hit the high points, yet cover a lot of ground.

Prescriptive — A prescriptive presentation is tailored for a particular client. You prescribe a specific solution to meet the client's
needs, much as a physician would prescribe a specific medicine for a

patient. There are four steps in a prescriptive presentation: diagnosis, analysis of the situation, presenting the product, and service. In a prescriptive presentation, you are selling yourself as a competent professional who can meet the needs and wants of that client. Of the three types of presentations, prescriptive requires the most effort on the part of the salesperson, but it does the best job of building confidence and allowing you to sell exactly what's right for that client at that particular time.

Which type is best for you depends on your product or service and on your particular style of selling. Perhaps you will want to experiment with all three until you determine which works best for you or you may decide to combine them.

Regardless which type of presentation you employ, the first thing you must do is get and hold the buyer's attention. Using the following seven steps works well:

1. Involve the customer. Ask questions, or, if appropriate, let the customer hold the product.

2. Tell appropriate stories or anecdotes to get the customer's attention.

3. Refer to a need the customer has, and propose a solution.

4. Offer powerful evidence as to why the customer needs your product or service.

5. Display appropriate showmanship.

6. Offer testimonials where appropriate. Think back to our discussion of behavior types. Socializers love testimonials; Directors could care less. So use this approach wisely.

7. If possible, give a demonstration of your product or service.

Keep these seven steps in mind as you prepare your presentation, because you can't be successful until you've got the buyer's attention.

Once you have it, you need to be aware of what's going on in the buyer's mind. The major factor every buyer contemplates is *the relationship between price and value*.

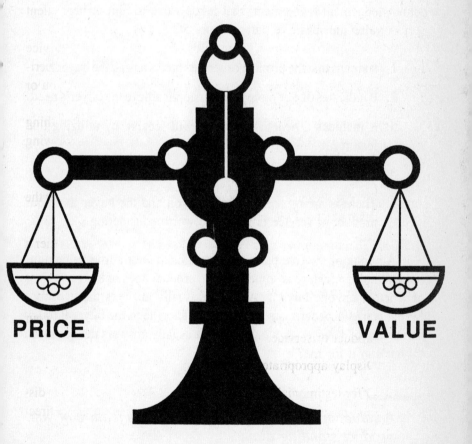

The buyer wants to know what's so great about your product or service that he or she should spend the money to buy it. The buyer wants to know that your product or service has what I call *value units*.

A value unit is a feature that your product or service offers shown in relationship with a need recognized by the buyer, along with proof that it will deliver the benefits as indicated, sealed by the buyer's acknowledgement (agreement) that it has value to him or her.

A value unit has five parts (Figure 5C):

1. It shows that the product or service meets a *need* the buyer has.

2. It indicates one or more *features* applicable to the buyer's need.

3. It includes a *benefit* the buyer will receive by utilizing that feature.

4. There is *proof* that the benefit will indeed come about.

5. There is an *agreement* between you and the buyer that your product or service is valid and worth considering.

Any one of the five parts working alone is not a true value unit. For example, a feature is something the product does or has regardless of whether anyone buys it. A feature usually answers the question, "What is it?" A benefit is a value that will accrue to the buyer through ownership of your product or service. It usually answers the question, "What's in it for me?"

A value unit is five times as powerful as feature of your product standing alone!

The buyer already knows price is on one side of the scale. Your job is to create value units in that client's mind so that the value of your product outweighs its price. Each time you build a value unit in the

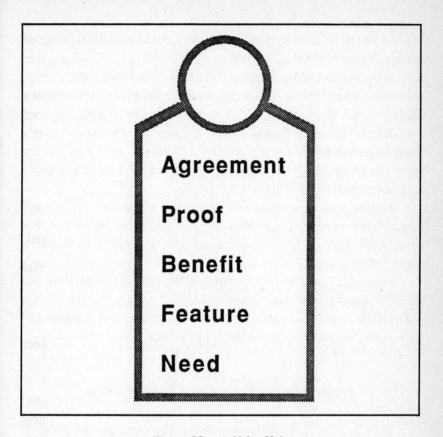

Figure 5C. A Value Unit

buyer's mind, it is placed on the scale automatically and weighed against the price required to buy.

When value outweighs price, the scales tip in your favor. You will know when this has happened, because the buyer will display a buying signal of some sort, either verbally or nonverbally.

When you see a buying signal, it's time to start wrapping up. Summarize the buyer's needs and the benefits you offer that address those needs, get the buyer to acknowledge that the two of you are in agreement, and ask for the order.

Present your product or service in such a way that the primary buying motives of that individual are addressed, one value unit at a time, until finally you see the scales tip. Try it out. I think you'll enjoy the benefits.

Figure 5D is a Feature-Benefit Worksheet that will help you identify reasons your customers would want to buy. Figure 5E is a Value Unit Worksheet that will allow you to diagram a number of value units for each customer need you identify.

Helpful Hints for a Good Presentation

Here is a list that briefly summarizes the suggestions for a good presentation discussed in this chapter:

- Trust the truth; don't overstate or understate.

- Be enthusiastic but not wild.

- Silence is OK sometimes.

- Make the warm-up natural.

- Present benefits in the buyer's order of importance.

- Confirm agreement early and often.

- Speak the buyer's language.

- When interrupted, review the last points.
- Reinforce the buyer's positive statements openly.
- Build only one value unit at a time.
- Stay buyer focused always.

FEATURE-BENEFIT WORKSHEET *

On this page list the major features of your product or service. After you have listed the features, list at least three benefits that accrue to the buyer from the use or ownership of that feature. After you complete the list, try to write down at least one advantage that each benefit offers to the buyer. The more clearly you define these here, the more powerful and convincing you will be when you are with the buyer.

FEATURE

1 _____

Benefits

1 _____
2 _____
3 _____

FEATURE

2 _____

Benefits

1 _____
2 _____
3 _____

FEATURE

3 _____

Benefits

1 _____
2 _____
3 _____

FEATURE

4 _____

Benefits

1 _____
2 _____
3 _____

FEATURE

5 _____

Benefits

1 _____
2 _____
3 _____

Figure 5D.   A Feature – Benefit Worksheet

*From Anthony Alessandra, Ph.D., La Jolla, CA.

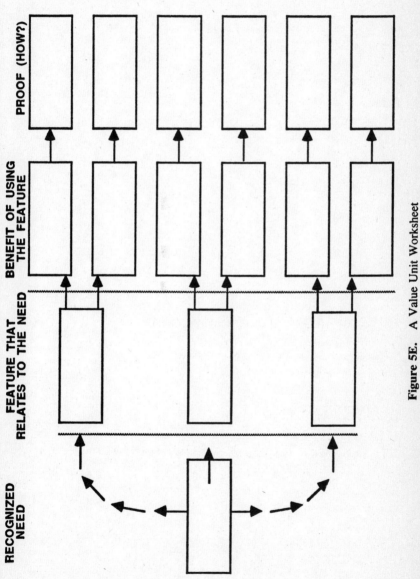

Figure 5E. A Value Unit Worksheet

Part Six

Confirming the Sale

People love to buy. We just have to allow them to participate in the sale and feel good about the choice they have made.

People love to buy. As salespeople, we don't have to force people to buy; we just have to allow them to participate in the sale and feel good about the choice they have made. Buyers want to buy; but before they do, they want to feel that they are in competent hands: yours. Buyers want a salesperson who shows leadership and is willing to guide them in the right direction.

As salespeople, when we fail to sell effectively, when we're not confident and well organized, we're cheating the buyer out of a feeling that he or she wants to have. Part of our job is to help the buyer to feel good about selecting our product or service.

> *There are three main reasons why people buy.*
>
> *1. They trust the seller.*
>
> *2. They like the product.*
>
> *3. The feel the product is worth the price.*

Isn't it interesting that number one is trust in the salesperson? As a salesperson, you are in a position to influence the buying decisions of your customer. If you are doing your job properly and professionally, influence is *not* manipulation. It is spending the time necessary to help that customer select the product or service that best meets his or her needs and wants.

The Three Elements of Persuasion

Persuasion in selling is nothing new. The Greek philosopher Aristotle named the three elements of persuasion in the third century B.C., describing them as:

Ethos — Character. In selling, you must first sell yourself to your customer. Let that customer know that you are worthy of his or her business.

Pathos — Feeling. People buy based on their feelings about a product or service. As a salesperson, you want to involve the customer's feelings in a positive and appropriate way.

Logos — Logic. People buy based on feeling, but they justify their buying decision on the basis of logic.

A combination of the three elements of persuasion is necessary for successful selling. You must present the right kind of logic so that customers can feel good about making a purchase. And you've got to sell yourself as the right person for the job.

Six Reasons People Don't Buy

Let's look at a few predictable reasons people don't buy:

Wrong seller	Wrong time
Wrong product	Wrong sales technique
Wrong price	Because they were *never asked!*

The first five are self-explanatory. The sixth is hard to believe, but true nevertheless.

Selling is a lot like being on a movie set where each actor or actress is waiting for a cue to speak or make the right move. If we as salespeople don't give the buyer the right cue to move forward with the sale, no sale will take place.

When you and the buyer are in agreement to go ahead with the sale, it's time to ask for the order and confirm the sale. Remember, we want to *confirm the sale*, not *close the customer*.

Recognizing the Best Time to Confirm the Sale

Let's briefly review the sequence of events we use in making a sale.

Reservoir — From a vast ocean of people, we compile our reservoir of target market prospects.

Inventory — We move a percentage of target market prospects into our inventory through qualifying.

Plan — Once we have qualified our inventory, we prepare to contact them.

Meet, Study, Propose — We next meet with the prospective client, study his or her needs and wants, and propose an appropriate solution.

Confirm — If our proposal has been on target, this is the time to ask for the order and confirm the sale. The tricky part here is knowing *when* to confirm.

It's time to confirm the sale when the customer gives you a *buying signal*, a sign that he or she is ready to buy.

> *A buying signal is anything the customer does or says that indicates he or she has taken* mental *ownership of the product or service.*

These signals usually occur rather suddenly and are noticed through a shift in the behavior of the buyer. They can be detected in both the body language and voice quality of the buyer. For example:

Posture — The customer moves to the front of the chair, opens up, and visibly relaxes.

Movements — The customer re-examines the product or materials, or touches the product for the first time in a long while.

Appearance — The customer smiles, becomes friendlier looking, and uses more eye contact.

Language — The words the customer uses change favorably. "If" changes to "when," and "your" changes to "my."

Again, a buying signal is anything the customer does or says that indicates he or she has taken mental ownersihp of that product or service. When you see a buying signal, you know value has outweighed price in the customer's mind. And that's your cue to start wrapping up the details and confirming the sale.

Confirming — A Natural Continuation

Confirming the sale should not be a major event in and of itself. It should be a natural continuation of your entire presentation. It *is* possible to oversell, so watch for those buying signals, and ask for the order in an appropriate and professional manner.

Throughout your conversations with a buyer, that buyer will give off a variety of signals that indicate how the conversation is going. Pay close attention to the signals you are getting from your customer (Figure 6A).

When the customer's behavior tells you "I am with you 100 percent," you are seeing a green light. This customer is letting you know that he or she not only likes your product or service, but really likes you as a person and truly wants to do business with you. When you see nothing but green lights in front of you, *ask for the order*.

When what you see is a mixture of messages in the person's behavior, you are seeing a yellow, or caution, light. The customer is saying one thing, but communicating something else on another level. The words may be right, but the customer's body language and speech pattern are telling you the opposite.

When you see a yellow light, you should be aware that something isn't quite right and you need to be careful. Be receptive to other points of view. Ask for the buyer's opinion rather than a firm commitment at that point. Don't try to overwhelm the buyer with fancy doubletalk. The proper and professional thing to do is take a few

Figure 6A.   The customer's signals

mental steps backward and ask questions until you're sure you're on the right track. Listen carefully to the buyer's concerns and continue to build more value units for your product or service.

A red light jumps right out at you. The customer gives you all kinds of signals that he or she is not ready to buy. When you see a red light, it's not the time to ask for the order. No sale will be made until the buyer's concerns are handled to his or her satisfaction.

When you see a red light, do not focus on the product. Focus instead on the results that customer will receive through the use of your product. Ask questions to uncover the customer's primary concern, and address that concern.

No matter what set of signals you get from a customer, remember to practice the Platinum Rule: Treat the buyer as he or she would like to be treated.

Talk to people in terms that have value to them.

Pay attention to your customer. Each customer has a personal idea of what is valuable.

The Nonresponder

Even if your customer appears to be giving you a red light for the moment, be glad you're getting some kind of signal. Signals give you something to work with and indicate to you which direction to take.

Studies have proven that the toughest customer is not the reluctant buyer but the total nonresponder. The nonresponder looks at you with a dead-pan face and refuses to give you any feedback as to how the sales presentation is going. This is especially tough to deal with, because you don't know how your message is being received. When you encounter a nonresponder, the best strategy is to talk slowly, ask more questions, and give the buyer time to respond. Present your material in a logical sequence, and focus more on the benefits to the buyer than on the features of the product.

Unfortunately, what usually happens when a salesperson meets a nonresponder is that the salesperson gets a little self-conscious and begins to talk faster. In an effort to get a response, the salesperson jumps around from thought to thought, asks fewer questions instead of more, and focuses on the product rather than the benefits. Sometimes the salesperson gets so flustered, he or she freezes up and can't remember any part of the sales presentation.

If you should find yourself dealing with a nonresponder, remember to stay calm, address the buyer in a professional and appropriate manner, and try to see things from the buyer's perspective. After the sales call analyze what you did right and what you did wrong, and keep those observations in mind when you make your next call. The more you practice this, the more confident you will become when dealing with a nonresponder.

Handling Buyer Concerns

Here are a few pointers on how to handle buyer concerns or objections, how to proceed if you meet someone who is not receptive to your approach:

1. **Relax**
   Don't jump into a response, a brief silence is okay. Take a moment to get reorganized, and pause before responding.

2. **Inquire**
   Find out what the buyer's real concern is. Be willing to ask questions and listen to the answers. Give the buyer a chance to communicate his or her feelings.

3. **Determine the true concern**

Sometimes there are underlying fears or the buyer is confused about what you are really offering. Take the time to sort out any confusion or misunderstanding.

4. **Respond**

Respond to the buyer's fears in a calm, appropriate, and professional manner. Use your best value units in a structured response. Do not be condescending to your customer.

5. **Check**

After you have responded, check to see if your response was on target. If so, ask them to buy again and move forward. If not, go back through the steps once more.

In traditional selling, a buyer's concern is typically referred to as an "objection." In Relationship Selling, a concern is not viewed as something negative to be brushed off as quickly as possible. Instead, a concern is something the buyer wants addressed, before going on to the next step.

There are five major concerns that you are likely to encounter:

1. **No need**

The client doesn't think he or she needs your product or service. Show how your product or service will be valuable to the client, personally or in business. Focus on the benefits to the client, not on the product.

2. **No trust**

The client doesn't feel confident in you or your product. When you encounter this concern, stop and ask yourself if you are selling to the client the way he or she wants to be sold to. Check to be sure that you're actively bringing the tension level down for both of you.

3. **No interest**

If the buyer seems uninterested, it usually means that you haven't connected the buyer personally with the product or service. Answer the WIIFM question for them, "What's in it for me?" Arouse the buyer's curiosity. Get that buyer involved with the product or service in a personal way.

4. **No hurry**

The "I want to think about it first" response is sometimes a sign that clients are in no hurry to buy. They may agree that you have a great product or service, but they're in no rush. Show them the benefits of buying now or the dangers of delay.

5. **No ability**

The client can't afford to buy or wants to bring in someone else to make the final decision. When you encounter this response, determine whether it's a matter of not being able to afford your product or service at all, or whether the client just can't buy right at that moment. If the client really can't afford to do business with you, let it go for now and check back in a few months. On the other hand, if the stumbling block seems to be a temporary cash flow problem, you can *presell*. Make the sale today, but arrange for payment and delivery on a later date.

The Language of Selling

Whenever you speak with a potential buyer, use appropriate sales language. Use words that will entice the buyer, but don't make yourself sound like a snake-oil salesman. "Free," "new," "improved," "guaranteed," "latest," and "best" are all words that appeal to the prospective buyer, but use them only where appropriate.

Also, use words that will put the buyer at ease and make him or her feel good about making a purchase. For example, use the word "invest" instead of "buy," "eager" instead of "anxious," and "emphasize" instead of "stress." The words "anxious" and "stress" create tension in the buyer's mind, whereas "eager" and "emphasize" offer encouragement and make the buyer feel good about the purchase.

Structured Responses to Buyer Concerns

Let us assume for a moment that you're on a sales call, and even though you have made every effort to involve the customer and use appropriate sales language, you are still encountering buyer concerns. I have found the following seven responses to be very helpful in dealing with buyer concerns. Try working a few of them into your presentation when faced with one of the five concerns.

1. **Feel/Felt/Found or Think/Thought/Found**

   Here are some examples: "I understand how you *feel*" (I'm empathizing with you). "Many people have *felt* the same way" (That gives you the feeling that you are not alone in all this). "However, they have *found* that . . ." (and you then present your solution). This could be offered in this way; "I understand your *thinking*. I *thought* the same thing when I first saw this product. However, I have *found* that . . ."

2. **Convert to a question**

   When the customer makes a statement, many times it is difficult to rebut it. However, you can convert the statement into a question that allows you to answer it more easily. Example: "I don't think I could use that product." Your response could be: "There is an important question I perceive in your statement and that is 'How can you gain maximum use from a product like this?'" Then you proceed to answer the *question*, not rebut the statement.

3. **Echo technique**

   Sometimes you are faced with a response that really doesn't give you enough information. In this case you can reflect or echo it back to the prospect. The customer might say that the price is too high. Here, you can respond by saying, "Too high?" She or he will generally respond at that point by giving you more feedback and information. From there, you can address the concern about price from his or her perspective.

4. **Lowest common denominator**

   In this case you take a concern that has a big image in the buyer's mind and reduce it to a figure much easier to comprehend and handle. Example: "$300 is too much." Response: "$300 does seem like a large price tag until you consider that you will probably be using this 3,000 times a year, which means that your cost per usage is only 10 cents, a small price to pay for the increased convenience and profitability that comes from this product."

5. **Boomerang technique**

   Think of a boomerang and what it does. Once thrown, it makes a wide arc and then comes immediately back to the individual who threw it. You do this same thing with a buyer's concern. He says, "I'm too busy right now to implement this." You reply, "That is probably the main reason you should purchase it today." His response: "What?!" Your response: "The fact that you are too busy today means that you need more-than-ever the time savings that will come to you as a result of using our product. So implementing this today will alleviate your problem of not having enough time. It will actually give you more time to be more productive."

6. **Change the base**

   In this case you take the basis upon which the customer is founding a response and change it so that he or she can see things in a different light. Example: The person says, "This won't accomplish the ABC process." Your response: "The main reason that you had inquired about this product was increased convenience. An added benefit, naturally, would be that it would accomplish the ABC process, but the point to bear in mind is that it does bring you the convenience that you require and, therefore, the ABC process should be secondary to any other considerations."

7. **Compensation technique**

Sometimes a concern is based on a very real product short-coming that must be acknowledged. For example, a person might say, "This unit is too large for the space available." You could reply by saying, " I agree that it is larger than the space currently available, but the benefits of this product are so great that it would be unfair to deny yourself the benefits simply for the inconvenience of having to find a new space in which to put it." In this case, what you have done is say: "I agree that it is too big for that space, but the benefits of the product overpower that shortcoming, so let's go ahead with the purchase."

Sometimes you can use the classic "Ben Franklin Balance Sheet." To use this technique, you take a sheet of paper, divide it down the center and put "reasons for" on the left side and "reasons against" on the right side. Then you go down the sheet listing reasons for going ahead with the purchase and reasons against going ahead with the purchase. You add as much as you can to the reasons for going ahead with the purchase and then you acknowledge those things that have been stated as reasons against. It quickly becomes obvious to people whether they should go ahead or not. This written "balance sheet" can persuade many clients to go ahead.

Remember, buyer concerns are not objections. They are legitimate questions that deserve your attention and respect. Think back to the price-value scales. When you help the buyer build value units by answering their questions and meeting their concerns, the scales will begin to tip in your favor. You will find that your work becomes easier, you'll love what you're doing, and you'll be making a lot more sales.

Persevere

When the relationship is right, the details are negotiable. If the trust level between you and the buyer is high and if your intention is genuinely to be of service, there's no reason to let buyer concerns prevent the sale. You must learn to resist, assist, and persist:

1. **Resist**

    Resist the temptation to back off too early when faced with a concern. Hang in there. Also resist the temptation to take the easy sale and not press on to fully solve the buyer's problem.

2. **Assist**

    Assist the customer in defining his or her real needs. Help him or her understand the basic problem that stimulated the concern. Don't just relate to the concern itself, but rather to the issue that really prompted it. Also, assist the person after the sale in gaining the maximum benefits from the product or service you have delivered. Follow up and follow through.

3. **Persist**

    Persist in a way that shows that you genuinely care and you do want to be of service. Use the techniques described. When you persist without the intention of manipulating, you nonverbally convey your concern and your sincerity. This strengthens that trust bond even further.

As you go down that road of communication in the sales process and encounter those concerns, your knowledge, skills and intentions will allow you to choose the right path — the path to increased sales and increased personal satisfaction.

Part Seven

Assuring Customer Satisfaction

More business is lost every year through neglect than through any other cause. Customer satisfaction is not just an academic courtesy. It is vital to your business success.

In the late 1970s, a company called Technical Assistance Research Programs, Inc. did a study on consumer complaint behavior. They found that the average business never hears from ninety-six percent of its dissatisfied customers! For every complaint businesses did receive, there were another twenty-six customers with problems, and at least six of those were serious problems.

Even more important, the study revealed that on the average each dissatisfied customer tells from nine to twenty other people about his or her dissatisfaction!

Think about those numbers for a moment. More business is lost every year through neglect than through any other cause. Customer satisfaction is not just an academic courtesy. It is vital to your business success.

Service After the Sale

Service after the sale is the key to keeping your customers year after year. The way to recognize a true sales professional is to look at what he or she does *after* the sale.

A recent market research poll indicated that it is five times more expensive to generate new customers than to keep existing ones. Servicing the account is what keeps your buyers coming back, and it's certainly what separates the professional from the mediocre salesperson.

In building your business, you can service your existing clients or you can try to get new ones to replace the ones you've lost through neglect. When you think about all the work you did to build your reservoir and inventory and to move your customers through the sales pipeline, it just doesn't make sense to neglect them after a sale and have to do all that work all over again.

Your attitude during the delivery of the product or service can generate new sales for you without the need for extra sales calls, *if* you indicate a genuine interest in the well-being of that client. On the other hand, if you act as though servicing the client is a waste of your valuable time, that client will feel abandoned, and the trust he or she had in you will vanish. The next time the client wants to buy, another salesperson who has the client's interests at heart will look far more appealing.

The most successful salespeople don't just sell their product or service, they *install* it after the sale. No matter what your line of business, devise a way to make your client feel comfortable with the product or service after the sale. Consider the following examples for installing a product or service:

1. If you sell real estate, give your buyer an owner's manual for the new home. Show the buyer where the gas, water, and electric switches are. Prepare a list of important phone numbers. Give the buyer a map of the area and indicate the location of nearby schools, churches, and stores.

2. If you sell automobiles, take time to show the buyer how to operate the new car. Go over the manufacturer's manual, and be willing to answer questions the buyer may have.

3. If your product is clothing, show the customer how to use accessories with the purchase to create a different look.

4. If you sell insurance, prepare a summary which emphasizes that this wasn't a one-time purchase and that as their insurance needs change over the years, you'll be there to provide guidance and to suggest the policy that is just right for that customer.

> *The key to continued success is showing the customer how to maximize the use of whatever was purchased.*

If you sell a service, introduce the client to others in your office so that when the client calls, he or she is not talking to a stranger, but to a familiar member of the team.

Customers Are Members of Your Club

Think of your customers as members of your club. When someone buys from you, he or she has bought more than just a product or service. That customer has bought a membership in your personal club. As members of your club, your customers deserve two things: *recognition* and *special treatment*. If you treat your customers appropriately and give them the good service they deserve, they will reward you with continuous business throughout your sales career.

Think of a few ways to acknowledge your appreciation to the members of your club. Sometimes one sincere gesture can pay off more handsomely than tens of thousands of dollars' worth of organized promotion. An appropriate personal touch will always be appreciated by your customers. Try some of the following suggestions:

1. Send a little note to let your customers know you're thinking about them and to encourage them to call you if they have any questions.

2. Send a clipping from a newspaper or a magazine article you think they may enjoy.

3. Send holiday, birthday, or special event cards.

4. Make a notation of the names of your client's spouse and children, and refer to them by name in a phone call or letter.

Think of other things you can do specific to your industry that would be an appropriate acknowledgment to your customers.

Account Reviews

A regular account review is an excellent way to keep in touch with your regular customer and let them know you are interested in their success and well-being. Set up a tickler file to keep track of all the notes about your key accounts and personal items to review before each sales call. Include the client's name (and its pronunciation), names of family or friends, special dates or birthdays, and anything else you care to note to help you relate to this person.

On a regular basis, (annually, monthly, or semiannually), hold a formal account review to determine how your product or service is working for that customer. I recommend the following guidelines for setting up an account review with your clients:

1. Review their original purpose for becoming a customer. Re-establish what it was that brought that customer to you in the first place.

2. Determine what their experience was when they first started using your product or service. Did they find it helpful? Were there any problems? Were those problems solved?

3. Determine what their experiences were after they had been using your product or service for some time.

4. Review their experience with service and questions. Do they like the service they've been getting? Are they ready to expand? Do they have additional questions?

5. Do a new diagnosis of their needs. Determine what direction they plan to take in the future.

6. Write a new prescription. Determine how you can meet their needs for the future.

You can use a form like the one shown in Figure 7A to help with an account review.

I think more sales are lost each year through neglect than for any other reason.

Yearly Account Review Discussion Guide*

CLIENT: _____

1. Overall relationship between client and us:

2. How well do we keep the client informed:

3. Client's evaluation of our product knowledge and skill:

4. Accessibility of our key people:

5. Are we meeting the client's real needs and wants:

6. What are the strengths of our company:

7. What are the weaknesses of our company:

8. How does the client describe our company to friends:

9. Does the client understand our pricing and billing procedures:

10. How can we work better:

Figure 7A.   An Account Review Form

*From *The Business of Selling*, Alessandra & Cathcart, Prentice-Hall

Salespeople are notorious for making great sales and then dropping the ball. They don't provide the follow-through necessary to service the account and secure the customer's loyalty.

Lasting Sales Relationships

Building lasting sales relationships is one of the most beneficial things you will ever do as a salesperson. It's easier and more profitable to take care of the accounts you have than to put all your effort into digging up new ones every month or every year.

To help you build those lasting relationships, I encourage you to apply the KIORG formula, a guide that will take you beyond the range of the average salesperson and allow you to become a true professional. KIORG is not a real word, but it's a good memory tool because it helps you remember the key words in developing lasting client relationships.

K — Know your clients as individuals, not just as customers, but as people. Get to know their hobbies or personal interests. No one is at work twenty-four hours of every day. Find out what they care about and like to do in their free time.

I — Identify what each client is good at, what he or she is fascinated by, and what he or she values. If you know what your clients do well, then you can help them do it better. You can't go wrong by taking an interest in your clients.

O — Orient your clients to your company, yourself, and the team they will be dealing with when they do business with you. Make them feel they are calling a friend when they call you or your office.

R — Relate the ideas you present to the strengths and uniqueness of each client. Discover what the client's goals are, and relate your product or service to each client's chosen direction.

G — Guide your clients' growth as individuals and as companies. When you know how to help clients get to where they want to be, you are more than a salesperson; you are a valuable member of their team. You are a business advisor, and you have joined their unofficial board of advisors.

A true professional sells in such a way that everyone involved comes out a winner. The key ingredient in Relationship Selling is the relationship between the buyer and the seller. Let your customers know that when they buy a product or service from you, they get you and your service after the sale as part of the deal.

Own Your Own Sales Career

The way to be truly successful is to think like the owner of your own sales career. When you build a long-term perspective into your sales relationships, you are thinking like a business owner, because you're thinking about the marketing, the sales, and the follow-through service. This is what really separates the professional from the salesperson who is just doing a job.

Ask yourself, "How would the person I would like to be do the things I'm about to do?" When you can identify what it is that you want out of your career, you will take on the actions and behavior of that person you want to become. When you make an effort to practice Relationship Selling, the rewards will be there waiting for you. Your self-esteem will increase, your list of customers will increase, and your sales will increase.

Part Eight

How To Become Your
Own Sales Manager

Excellent salespeople think and act as the owners of their careers.

Have you ever thought about what qualities separate the true winners in any field from the rest of the group? The truly successful salespeople are the ones who go the extra mile and set themselves apart from the crowd.

Excellent salespeople have a philosophy that elevates them above those who are just doing a job.

> *Excellent salespeople think and act as the owners of their careers. Mediocre salespeople think and act merely as representatives of their firm.*

To visualize yourself as the owner of your own sales career, fill in the blanks in this exercise:

> *The _____(your name)_____ Company*
>
> *Providing a_____(type of business)_____ service*
>
> *Currently under contract with ____(name of firm)____ .*

How does the above description affect the way you think about yourself and the job you hold as a salesperson?

Qualities of a Professional

When you operate as the owner and manager of your own sales career, it's important to remember that the value of your company tomorrow will be determined by the habits you cultivate today. A professional looks like a professional, and this includes behavior, not just physical appearance. When you meet with a client, look and act the way your customer thinks you should look and act. Keep your car clean and your office tidy. Papers scattered everywhere make the customer think you are disorganized, even untrustworthy. Think back to the price versus value scale. *Sell yourself as a professional.*

Develop a strategy and tactic for managing your accounts, your territory, and yourself. Remember, your customers are members of *your* club. Only your positive attitude toward your clients as human beings will ensure the mutual trust that is so vital to your success.

Professionalism is a state of mind and conduct. Taking pride in yourself and in what you do is the seed from which professionalism grows.

> *Whether a person is a professional isn't determined by the business he or she is in, but by the way he or she is in business.*

It's easy to spot a person who has a clearly defined set of goals. That person exudes a sense of purpose and determination. When you carry that attitude, you will be rewarded with a profitable and fulfilling career.

Why Have You Chosen Sales?

To be successful in sales, you have to be in the selling field because you *want* to be in that field. That's the best motivation in the world. Take a moment to read The Salesperson's Oath in Figure 8A and review why it is that you have chosen this noble profession.

A truly professional and successful salesperson thinks not only like the owner of his or her business, but like the owner of the *client's* business. A true professional always has the client's best interest at heart and wants to see the client be successful. This is the hallmark of *we*-oriented thinking. Both the buyer and the seller come out as winners.

The Salesperson's Oath

I choose to be a professional in the field of selling. I make this choice knowing that selling has many requirements.

Selling requires caring. In order to truly serve others and to help people own the right product or service to fill their needs, I must learn to identify their needs. I must be skilled in the twin arts of probing and listening, for one without the other is useless.

Selling requires planning and study. For my sales career to endure, it must be built upon a foundation of solid planning for long-term and short-term success. I must study my products and services until I know them thoroughly. I must know exactly how my customer can benefit most from the use of my products or services. I must study the selling skills that will allow me to help my customer own the right product for his or her needs.

Selling requires strength of character. There will be times when I am tempted to make an easy sale that does not benefit the customer. At these times I must have the strength of character to avoid the sale and act in my customer's best interests. I must be able at all times to say that I have advised the customer to do exactly what I would do if I were in his or her position.

Selling requires determination and persistence. Some people will not see the immediate value of buying from me. I must persist tactfully in helping them to understand how I can be of service. Many on whom I call will not buy my products. I must believe unflinchingly in the law of cause and effect (every good act brings a reward; every bad act brings a consequence). If I make enough calls on qualified customers with a professional attitude, I will achieve my goals.

Selling is dependent on the free enterprise system and is an integral part of it. Selling is based on the premise that one person's knowledge, skills, and handiwork can benefit another. It is further based on the belief that one should be compensated for providing a service. Profit is the incentive that motivates improvement and increase. Profit, whether financial or otherwise, is part of ownership, and with ownership there is always responsibility.

Selling requires responsibility. I must recognize my responsibility to serve my client well, uphold the principles of this oath and my profession, improve my own knowledge and skills, and profit from my labors. When I earn it, it is my right, for I am a professonal salesperson. In today's society, a professional is not measured by the business he or she is in, but by the way he or she does business.

© 1987 Jim Cathcart, Inc.

Figure 8A. The Salesperson's Oath

Professionals share certain traits that constantly contribute to their success. Professionals are:

1. **Committed to personal growth**

   To be successful, you must know where you're going in life; you must set goals. Take the time to write out your goals, and you'll be surprised at what a difference it will make.

2. **Coachable**

   Professionals are willing to take direction from another person, willing to listen and learn how to improve their own skills and techniques.

3. **Willing to pay their dues**

   Successful salespeople are willing to take the time to learn the ins and outs of the sales profession. They're not just looking for the one big sale before they're off to something else. They're in this for the long haul.

4. **Nonblamers**

   Professionals don't have time to blame other people for any setbacks or mistakes. They're too busy moving forward to carry around old baggage of wants and wishes. They take personal responsibility for both their successes and their failures.

5. **Supporters and givers**

   Professionals are willing to share their ideas and techniques with others because they know that when others are successful, it's a win for the entire selling profession.

6. **Aware of the "score."**

   Winners always keep score. They know where their career is going at all times. They keep accurate records. They know what's working and what needs work.

Think about what your time is worth to you every day, and then spend that time where it will be most productive.

As Figure 8B shows, the more selling time in your day, the more income it will produce.

Figure 8C is an exercise that can help you set priorities for the way you spend your time.

Selling by the Numbers

I want to share with you a concept I call *Selling by the Numbers*. It will help you to know what is working for you and what to do if you want to change the results of your production. In other words, it will tell you how to make more money and be more successful.

To assist you with your record keeping, set up a file with the categories listed below:

Inventory	These are the potential buyers you have qualified from your reservoir. You draw on this inventory to make your contacts.
Calls	Record the attempts you make on a daily basis to get in touch with someone in your inventory.
Contacts	When you actually connect with the desired person or decision maker you have been calling record it here.
Interviews	Record your face-to-face meetings to discuss business.
Sales attempts	These are meetings at which you asked the person to buy.

Sales	When you've actually confirmed a deal and taken an order for your product or service, record it here.
$ Value of each sale	Your commission or profit from each sale.
Retention percentage	Compute the percentage of customers who stay with you after the initial purchase.

What Your Time Is Worth **Based on Yearly Income**		
*Yearly Income**	*Every Hour Is Worth* *(40 Hr. Week)*	*1 hr/wk of* *Selling Time* *Is Worth*
$ 5,000	$ 2.56	$ 128.00
$ 7,500	$ 3.84	$ 192.00
$ 10,000	$ 5.12	$ 256.00
$ 20,000	$10.25	$ 512.50
$ 30,000	$15.37	$ 768.50
$ 40,000	$20.50	$1,025.00
$ 50,000	$25.62	$1,281.00
$ 60,000	$30.74	$1,537.00
$ 70,000	$35.86	$1,793.00
$ 80,000	$40.94	$2,047.00
$ 90,000	$46.10	$2,305.00
$100,000	$51.23	$2,561.00

*Based on approximately 50 working weeks per year.

Figure 8B.   The Value of Your Time

From *The Business of Selling*, Alessandra & Cathcart, Prentice-Hall

---

High-Priority Activities *

DIRECTIONS: List below the six most important, high-payoff activities you
perform on the job in the eyes of your immediate manager, your
clients or customers, and yourself. Then, come up with the
overall top six activities regardless of individual perspective.

In the eyes of my immediate manager:
1.
2.
3.
4.
5.
6.

In the eyes of my clients/customers/prospects:
1.
2.
3.
4.
5.
6.

In my own eyes:
1.
2.
3.
4.
5.
6.

The overall high-priority activities:
1.
2.
3.
4.
5.
6.

Figure 8C.   An Exercise for Prioritizing Activities

*From *The Business of Selling*, Alessandra & Cathcart, Prentice-Hall

Now imagine that you have started a new discipline of keeping records on these activities every day. Let's say you know where you stand in each category, and you want to make some improvements.

If you notice from your records that your *inventory is getting low*, it indicates that you aren't doing enough of the right kind of prospecting and target marketing. New names must be added from the reservoir every week.

If you're *not making enough calls*, that usually indicates poor time management. Go over your daily records and see where you are spending your time. Watch for culprits like spending too much time deciding whom to call, or too much time traveling between calls, or too much time at the water cooler. Are you calling each client at the best time of day to reach that client? Not the best time of day for yourself, but the best time for *that client*. If not, why not?

If you're making lots of calls but *not making many contacts*, somehow you are calling on the wrong people, or at the wrong time, or you are calling in the wrong way.

If you're *not getting many interviews*, there may be a problem in the way you are trying to sell the interview. Check your opening statements and the benefits you are promising. Make sure you are building trust throughout this phase.

If you're getting the interviews, but find you have *few actual sales attempts relative to the number of interviews* you've been getting, the problem could be that you lack the confidence to ask for the order. Have you cheated on the study phase? Do you not fully understand the client's situation and goals? If so, that could be why you are reluctant to sell. Remember to give the client time to talk so you can gather more information about his or her company. Then, when you know you have a firm grasp on the situation, ask for the order.

Now let's look at the bottom line. You've obtained the interview and asked for the order, but you're just *not making the sales*. Why? It could be that there is something wrong with the way you are asking. Either you are putting on too much pressure or not enough. Or perhaps your offer is not right for the needs and wants of that buyer. Check to be sure that you are really making the best offer for that person at that time. Remember, prescription before diagnosis is malpractice.

If the *dollar value of your sales is too low*, you may be working the wrong market or not filling all the needs of the customer. Don't settle for the easy sale. Probe to uncover additional needs and wants, and convince your customer of the importance of filling them now.

If you are making initial sales, but the *customers are soon leaving you for someone else*, something is seriously wrong. It could be that your product or service doesn't live up to your claims. But unless that's a proven fact, it's more likely that something is wrong with the way you sell. Go back and read this book carefully. Make notes and work on your sales technique. Above all, concentrate on your service *after* the sale. There is no substitute for customer satisfaction.

Read the Sales Consultant's Checklist in Figure 8D. As you read the list, check yourself, noting the areas that need attention.

Well, how did you do? The answers which were not acceptable to you will show you where additional work is required. Your next step is to write out a plan of action for when and how you will address each of the needs.

After you have accumulated thirty to sixty days of accurate records, you will know where your strengths are and where you need to do some work. If you work diligently at this project, you will soon be able to write your own paycheck for whatever amount you want to make as a professional salesperson.

No matter which technique you choose to employ to achieve your own selling goals, you must truly believe in yourself and in what you are doing to be successful. Every day ask yourself, "How would the person I would like to be do the things I'm about to do?" When you live up to the standards you have set for yourself, you will truly be your own sales manager.

Good selling.

Sales Consultant's Checklist

1. Am I aware of the targeted market segments that best meet my firm's purpose and objectives?

2. Do I have written goals and objectives for sales accomplishments and self-development?

3. Are specific goals established for each client contact or sales call?

4. Have I written out my objectives for the development of each existing account?

5. How do I prepare for each sales call?

6. Are clear, up-to-date records kept to show the ratio of calls to interviews to sales, and so forth?

7. How much time each day is actually devoted to **selling** (personal contact with potential buyers)?

8. Am I confident, professional, and appropriate in the initial contact with clients?

9. Do I know what questions to ask to clearly define potential client needs?

10. Do I ask the questions in a way that encourages full disclosure and trust from the client?

11. Do I restate the needs and wants as I understood them, to verify them with the client?

12. Do I translate the features of my product or service into benefits desired by the client?

13. Are my responses to client concerns and objections calm and appropriate?

14. Am I clear and tactful when asking for the order?

15. Do I summarize benefits and needs before asking the client to buy?

16. Once the sale is confirmed, do I review the details and describe what happens next?

17. Do I follow through to assure that the client gets the benefits he or she was seeking?

18. Do I stay in touch with clients regularly (or only when I want another sale)?

Figure 8D.   A Checklist for Effective Sales

Powerful Thoughts for Relationship Selling

1. In selling as in medicine, prescription before diagnosis is malpractice!

2. When the relationship is right, the details are negotiable. When tension is high, the details become obstacles.

3. When there is not much difference between your product and that of your competitors, there had better be a big difference in the way you deal with people.

4. We judge ourselves by our intentions, but others judge us by our actions.

5. Motivation is like bathing. It may not last, but it's still a good idea now and then.

6. Whether a person is professional is no longer determined by the business he or she is in, but rather by the way that person is in business.

7. The Platinum Rule: Do unto others as they would have you do unto them.

8. If you want to improve your circumstances, begin by improving yourself.

9. It is impossible to avoid leading by example. Somebody is always watching.

10. Maturity is being able to get yourself to do what needs to be done when it needs to be done whether you feel like it or not, and still doing it well.

11. Worrying is mentally rehearsing disaster.

Powerful Thoughts for
Relationship Selling (continued)

12. Become the kind of person who would achieve your goals, and the accomplishment of the goals will be the natural by-product.

13. People will teach you how to deal with them if you'll pay attention to the messages they are sending.

14. Sometimes one sincere gesture can do more for your business than thousands of dollars worth of advertising.

15. It's not just whether you sell the right item that counts. It's whether the customer *realizes* that it was the right item.

16. The best way to get what you want is by helping others get what they want.

17. People don't care what you know until they know that you care.

18. Your pay will always be roughly equal to the contribution you are making. To give yourself a raise, make a greater contribution to others.

19. Successful salespeople think and act as the owners of their careers.

20. There are no traffic jams in the extra mile.

Additional Resources from Jim Cathcart
for Enhancing Your Skills

Trainer's Manual

Mastering Relationship Selling.   A 100-page trainer's manual and coaching guide designed to make *Relationship Selling* easy to teach and manage. Contains sixty-seven easy-to-lead exercises from fifteen minutes to one hour in length. Also contains a complete cross reference for the book contents along with specific steps for teaching each skill covered in the book. Can be expanded or simplified easily by the sales trainer or manager.

Audio Cassette Albums

Super Star Selling: How to Manage Your Way to Seven Figure Sales by Jim Cathcart and Tony Alessandra (a 6-tape album). Learn how to dominate your industry by outselling the competition. Covers marketing, competitive analysis, negotiating, prospecting, and getting maximum results from your sales time (published by Nightingale—Conant).

The Acorn Principle by Jim Cathcart (a 6-tape album). The messages on these audio cassettes are filled with profound information on: Finding your natural intelligence, understanding your natural values, sustaining your optimum velocity, managing your personality patterns, identifying and clarifying your sense of purpose, attaining mastery in all that you pursue, passing these gifts along to others, achieving alignment in relationships and lifestyle, learning to live fully in all that you do. A comprehensive course in self-awareness.

Videotapes

Rethinking Sales. A live presentation by Jim Cathcart explaining the concept, techniques and philosophy of the book *Relationship Selling.* Entertaining and motivational. A good overview of the concept and material.

Rethinking Yourself. In this presentation, Jim Cathcart shares the wisdom of The Acorn Principle "Your greatest, fastest and easiest growth always comes from your natural abilities." A live keynote speech delivered before more than one thousand professional speakers at their annual convention. Highly motivational.

Helping People Grow. One hour of Jim Cathcart's most powerful ideas on how to get the most from yourself and others. Plenty of meat and plenty of humor. For leaders and parents.

Video-Based Training Programs

The Relationship Selling Library. Several hours of video and audio training covering every aspect of sales. Leader's guide included. This is the entire course that goes with the book *Relationship Selling.* Can be blended with other programs or used by itself as a complete course.

Book

The Sales Professional's Idea-a-Day Guide by Tony Alessandra, Gregg Baron and Jim Cathcart. A 365-page workbook. Easy-to-use reference for getting a new idea or double-checking ones you haven't used in a while. The most flexible and usable sales book you'll ever own. Contains more than 100 worksheets to help organize your thoughts and ideas and put them into action, and 250 separate ideas with exercises. A perfect year-long training course.

Be Your Own Sales Manager by Tony Alessandra, Jim Cathcart and John Monoky. A powerful how-to book which will give you complete control over your career and your accounts (published by Prentice Hall).

For detailed information about these products and Jim Cathcart's presentations, call or write to:

Jim Cathcart
P O Box 9075
La Jolla, CA 92038

toll free (800) 222-4883
fax (619) 456-7218

on-line: www.cathcart.com

About the Author
Jim Cathcart, CSP, CPAE

In 1972, Jim Cathcart was working as a clerk in Little Rock, Arkansas. Five years later he was traveling the world as a professional speaker and sales trainer. Today, with over twenty years of intense study in the field of human interaction, Jim is one of the most popular sales trainers in the world.

He has trained over two thousand audiences to use his techniques for growing more business. Using his techniques, one of his clients raised sales from $17 million to over $231 million! Jim has personally earned several million dollars in speaking fees and was chosen 1988–89 president of the National Speakers Association.

Jim's other works include *Super Star Selling, The Sales Professional's Idea-a-Day Guide, Be Your Own Sales Manager*, and *The Acorn Principle*.

In 1985, Jim received the Council of Peers Award for Excellence (CPAE) bestowed by the National Speakers Association. Other recipients include President Ronald Reagan, Dr. Norman Vincent Peale, Earl Nightingale and Zig Ziglar.

When he isn't traveling the world working to increase his client's sales and personal success, Jim lives in beautiful La Jolla, California, with his wife and son.